THE CURE

Once you accept that you're

terminally ill, you'll do whatever

it takes to find the cure.

THE
CURE
PRESCRIPTION FOR LIFE

STEVE BYRENS

Ambassador International
GREENVILLE, SOUTH CAROLINA & BELFAST, NORTHERN IRELAND

www.ambassador-international.com

The Cure
Prescription for Life

ISBN: 978-1-62020-250-0
eISBN: 978-1-62020-350-7

Cover design and typesetting: Matthew Mulder
E-book conversion: Anna Riebe

AMBASSADOR INTERNATIONAL
Emerald House
427 Wade Hampton Blvd.
Greenville, SC 29609, USA
www.ambassador-international.com

AMBASSADOR BOOKS
The Mount
2 Woodstock Link
Belfast, BT6 8DD, Northern Ireland, UK
www.ambassadormedia.co.uk

The colophon is a trademark of Ambassador

I would like to dedicate this book to my wife Sonia. Not only did God use you to show me the power of His grace and love, but it was your belief in me that gave me the courage to start writing this book. I love you sweetheart!

WORD OF THANKS

I WOULD LIKE TO EXPRESS my deep gratitude to pastor Ray Pritchard (www.keepbelieving.com) for giving me his permission to extensively quote from his excellent sermon series on the Beatitudes. It was during the research stage for my own sermon series, which preceded the writing of this book, that I came across his work. Dr. Pritchard's illuminating scriptural insight was foundational in igniting my passion for this study of the Beatitudes.

CONTENTS

CHAPTER 1

THE DIAGNOSIS

THERE'S A HUMOROUS STORY TOLD about Muhammad Ali, that allegedly occurred during his reign as boxing's heavyweight champion of the world. As the story goes, Ali was returning from a business trip to Asia when his flight encountered extreme turbulence. After a few moments of violent shaking, the pilot came on the intercom ordering the passengers to return to their seats and fasten their seat belts. While the flight attendant was making her way through the plane, checking that each passenger had safely complied with the captain's orders, she noticed Ali defiantly standing in the aisle. Concerned for his safety, she approached him and asked, "Hey champ, why haven't you followed the captain's orders to sit down and fasten your seat belt?" Ali slowly turned his head and replied, "Superman don't need no seat belt." Without missing a beat, the attendant answered, "Well that may be true, but Superman don't need no airplane either! Now sit down and buckle up!"

This story helps to illustrate a key problem that all of us face in one way or another as fallen human beings. We have a tendency to exaggerate our own abilities, while at the same time underestimating the potential for danger in any given situation. If you don't believe me, think about the popularity of the television show *America's Funniest Home Videos*. How often do you tell yourself at the beginning of a video, "Oh no, this is not going to end well!" What makes a young person think he can jump a skateboard up onto a metal handrail that is over a long set of cement stairs, and not get hurt? What makes an adult (a person who has had a complete lifetime to watch and learn how the law of gravity works) think that he can somehow jump across a five-foot-wide river without falling in?

Whether we're willing to admit it or not, we all have a tendency to do this type of thing. I can remember leaving my sixth-hour class during high school so that I could jump into my best friend's truck and drive around the back roads that surrounded our small farm-town community, looking for cheap thrills as we killed time before football practice. On one occasion, we were going about 55 miles per hour around a curve on a dirt road, laughing and feeling invincible, when all of a sudden he lost control and we struck a tree. Thankfully, no one was hurt and we quickly realized just how close we had come to serious injury or even death. But just a few weeks later, the lesson seemed like a distant memory, and that old feeling of invincibility was back. That night, on a dare, we drove down another dirt road at an extremely high rate of speed with our headlights off and the interior lights on. When I think back on how foolish those actions were, I am convinced that there is something inside all of us (to one degree or another) that seems programmed to try and deny our personal weaknesses and vulnerabilities. We become so self-assured that we brazenly ignore the warnings of others who try to bring us back to reality. "Sure, I know this is dangerous, but don't worry; I can handle it." And as a result, we can spend long periods of time living under the illusion that we're invincible. This illusion continues until reality catches up with us, and we're forced to face the truth head-on. Like the examples I gave earlier, it might happen when you lose control of your truck and crash into a tree. It might happen when you and your skateboard fall off a metal hand-rail, causing you to break a bone on the cement below. It might even happen when you find yourself standing waist deep in a river that you were sure you could jump across. But even more signifi-cantly, you might have to face your weaknesses and vulnerabilities when your marriage begins to fall apart, when alcohol and drugs are the only way you can get through the day, when your paycheck is gone before the bills are paid, or when every relationship around you is broken and you suddenly realize you're the only common denominator in all of them.

Throughout human history, one of the biggest struggles man-kind has faced is the struggle to admit our need for God. We don't like the idea that we can't do it on our own. In Psalm 14:1–3, the psalmist warns us, "The fool says in his heart, 'There is no God.' They are corrupt, their deeds are vile, there is no one who does good. ²The LORD looks down from heaven on all mankind to see if there are any who understand, any who seek God. ³All have turned away, all have become corrupt; there is no one who does good, not even one." This text makes an extremely uncomfortable point to those of us who pride ourselves on the fidelity of our relationship to God. Whether we want to believe it or not, there are times in our lives when we're all guilty of forgetting about God, of trying to do things in our own strength and in our own way. Though we may not always deny Him with our lips, we often do so by our actions!

As much as evolutionists would love to make us believe that we are the masters of our own destinies, it is simply not true. We are all here by the grace and power of God. Everything we have is a gift from Him, and until we understand our need, along with God's provision for that need, we will continue to try and manage things that are well beyond our ability to control. We will live under the delusion that we are competent and in charge. But listen to what the Creator of the universe has to say concerning this important issue:

> I make known the end from the beginning, from ancient times, what is still to come. I say: "My purpose will stand, and I will do all that I please. From the east I summon a bird of prey; from a far-off land, a man to fulfill my purpose. What I have said, that will I bring about; what I have planned, that will I do." – Isa. 46:10–11

> As the rain and the snow come down from heaven, and do not return to it without watering the earth and making it bud and flourish, so that it yields seed for the sower and bread for the eater, [11] so is my word that goes out from my mouth: It will not return to me empty, but will accomplish what I desire and achieve the purpose for which I sent it. – Isa. 55:10–11

Go to Google Images and look at a picture of Muhammad Ali when he made his claim about being Superman. Then find a picture of him today, showing him after being ravaged by the effects of Parkinson's disease. Whether we are willing to admit it or not, none of us is Superman. We all have weaknesses and frailties, which may be covered up at the moment, but sooner or later they'll come out. And one of the most powerful illustrations available for demonstrating this truth can be seen when a person is confronted with a terminal disease.

A TERMINAL DISEASE

Every year in the US, 1.4 million people are given the news that they have cancer. Of that number, over five hundred thousand of them are told that it is terminal. Think about the impact of this diagnosis: one day you are living your life under the illusion that you are invincible; the next day you find out that you have cancer and that you are likely going to die. I have never been diagnosed with cancer. I've never had to sit in a doctor's office and have the doctor tell me that my tumor is malignant. But from talking with people who have, I know a process takes place in the human heart and mind that forces us to begin dealing with our own mortality.

Although not always exactly in this order, the process looks something like this:

1. denial: cancer is something that happens to other people;
2. what are my options: how can I take care of this problem and make it better?
3. re-evaluating priorities: if my time is limited, I want to start focusing on what's important;
4. acceptance and treatment: okay, I admit I can't handle this on my own, so I'm going to accept the treatments that are being offered.

Most of the time this means a complete life change: a new diet, a new set of habits, and ruthlessly getting rid of anything that might have contributed to the disease. A transformation takes place in how your priorities shape the way you live your life. When you boil it all down, you realize an important truth: you don't want to die, you want to live! At this point you are now ready and willing to do whatever takes to find the cure!

As a matter of fact, billions of dollars are raised every year by all sorts of organizations attempting to find the cure for cancer and other terminal diseases. The sad reality is that what we can see so clearly when it comes to our physical health, we reject when it comes to our spiritual health! We'll do almost anything to find a cure when we are sick. We'll get rid of food. We'll get rid of products that contain dangerous chemicals. We'll stay out of the sun. We'll submit our bodies to chemotherapy (actually shooting poison into your body to kill the cancer so that the rest of the body can live). We'll do whatever it takes to avoid the things that lead to cancer and physical death, and yet never give a second thought to the things all around us that lead to spiritual cancer and spiritual death.

What is very interesting to note is that while Jesus did much to help people who suffered physically, when it came right down to it, His main focus was spiritual life. Every time He healed a person, every time He cast out a demon, every time He provided food, it was always to open the person's eyes to their deeper need for God. Let's look at a couple of examples from the Bible:

> Jesus answered, "Everyone who drinks this water will be thirsty again, but whoever drinks the water I give them will never thirst. Indeed, the water I give them will

become in them a spring of water welling up to eternal life." – John 4:13–14

Meanwhile his disciples urged him, "Rabbi, eat something." But he said to them, "I have food to eat that you know nothing about." Then his disciples said to each other, "Could someone have brought him food?" "My food," said Jesus, "is to do the will of him who sent me and to finish his work." – John 4:31–36

In these verses, Jesus makes it clear that God knows we have physical needs, and that He is more than willing to meet those needs on our behalf. But His concern is that we spend so much of our time and energy trying to meet our physical needs, assuming that once we have met them, we'll then be happy and satisfied. We somehow convince ourselves that if we meet our physical appetites, we will also satisfy our spiritual hunger. But this just doesn't match up with reality. We live in one of the most wealthy and affluent cultures to ever exist on earth. A small minority of people in America are without access to everything they need to meet their basic physical needs. But satisfying physical needs can never take the place of satisfying our deeper spiritual hunger. If you don't believe me, watch one episode of *True Hollywood Story*. Do a little research on the average life expectancy of a childhood star. Even scarier, simply take a look at the deterioration of the families in your own community. Everywhere we look we see brokenness and despair. The rate of suicide among teenagers is skyrocketing. Drug and alcohol abuse are rampant. Traditional families are disintegrating. And large numbers of people are simply checking out of life!

As one person described to me recently, concerning her attempts to minister to some of the broken people who frequent the bank where she works, "Sometimes it feels like being in a movie, surrounded by zombies."

When our God-given spiritual needs go unmet, the result is a spiritual cancer—a disease of the soul that is just as fatal and just as deadly as any form of physical cancer. Proverbs 17:22 says, "A merry heart does good, like medicine, but a broken spirit dries the bones." We may not want to admit it, but we are all spiritually sick. There is a cancer spreading rapidly through our culture and we're all being directly affected! But like Muhammad Ali who thought he was Superman, like the kid on the skateboard who thought he could defy gravity, like my best friend who thought he was invincible driving the back roads—until someone can convince us we are sick and in need of a cure, we just keep trying to find our own answers; answers that continue to push us further from God and deeper into our own sicknesses of selfishness and pride.

Unfortunately, instead of turning to our Creator for answers, in our pride and arrogance we (mankind) have instead tried to solve the problem ourselves. After all, we are the smartest, most sophisticated culture to ever live, aren't we? We've been to the moon. We've defeated many diseases that plagued our ancestors. If we just try hard enough, surely we can find the cure for society's ills.

LOOKING FOR THE CURE

As Philip Keller points out in his wonderful book entitled *Salt For Society,* our culture has tried many different methods for solving this dilemma:

EDUCATION

If we just find a way to educate everyone, we tell ourselves, we can civilize them. When people are taught the basic subjects and learn how to reason through their problems, we think, we will no longer have conflicts and wars. Everyone will have everything they need to be happy. But these dreams turned out to be false hopes. In fact, they became false gods. Mankind continues to pour hundreds of billions of dollars into education, but it is an education stripped of any reference to God. Recent studies show that less than one percent of professors on college campuses in the West consider themselves to be Christian. Millions of students spend years acquiring knowledge that does not include an understanding of God and the key role He has played in human history. Their minds are fed, but their spirits are slowly starved.

ECONOMICS

We think if we can just build the perfect economic system, then all of mankind's problems can be fixed. After the Great Depression of the 1930's, the world's intellectual elite set their sights on developing the perfect economy. Everything from the New Deal to communism to fascism was held up as mankind's next great hope. But instead of setting mankind free, these systems led to a world-wide war, the death of over 200 million people, and mass destruction throughout Europe and Asia! Although Western society came out of this chaos with a system that has led to previously unheard of levels of affluence, interestingly, its people still feel a deep sense of emptiness and fear. With every new catastrophic event, it becomes more evident that this newfound wealth could simply disappear overnight.

POLITICS

Certainly, it was said, the answer would be found through international cooperation and world politics. The obvious solution to mankind's ills was to develop organizations like the United Nations, NATO, and the European Union. These great think tanks would surely be able to bring peace and prosperity to everyone equally. But instead of working together to solve our problems, each group has selfishly developed its own agenda. Sadly, these groups' agendas have been humanistic in nature, continuing to push broken people further and further from the help they need in God. And not too surprisingly, these groups are disintegrating before our very eyes.

SCIENCE

Give us enough well-trained minds, enough money, and enough research facilities, the scientists told us, and we'll come up with all the answers. But once again, human arrogance got in the way. Even though many of the scientific disciplines were first developed as a way to find out more about the God who created the world in which we live, today's scientific community has excluded any discussion of God. If God can't be measured, if He can't be subjected to the scientific process, then (so we are now told) He must not exist. In an interesting twist of irony, instead of solving mankind's problems, science has instead magnified them: by systematically diminishing the importance of God. Scientific invention apart from a reference to the character and nature of a holy God leads to devastating consequences. Some of the most destructive and horrific human devices ever created are now within the reach of thoroughly evil men: men who are willing to use them to reach their own selfish political agendas. Already in possession of large armies and devastating fire power, the leaders of rogue nations such as Iran and North Korea are on the verge of having nuclear weapons at their disposal.

When it comes to finding the cure for what ails the human heart, it has become self-evident that mankind's best efforts fall woefully short. Would it surprise you to know that this is nothing new? Three thousand years ago, King Solomon, the richest and wisest man who ever lived, wrote these words: "I have seen all the things that are done under the sun; all of them are meaningless, a chasing after the wind" (Eccles. 1:14). These are words spoken by a man who had all the resources and power to do anything he wanted with his life. Yet in the end, apart from a close personal relationship with God, he could not find the cure for the ache and brokenness of the human heart!

Now by this point I know what some of you may be thinking: "Geez, Steve, could you get any more depressing? I started reading this book looking for hope. But so far I don't see it!" Well, if that's the case, then I've done my job as a doctor. I've successfully brought you to the place in your diagnosis where you realize that you have a problem, and this problem is too big for you to handle on your own. You are not going to get better until you are willing to get help.

I WANT TO GET WELL!

As we discovered earlier, when a person finally accepts that he has a fatal disease, he becomes willing to do whatever it takes to find the cure for that disease. Ultimately, he becomes willing to do whatever it takes to get well.

People were no different two thousand years ago in the Middle East. Jesus walked into a culture full of people who suffered from the same problems we face in our culture; the people of Israel were just as broken and empty as we are today. Just like us, they had seen the failure of education, economics, government, and science to bring peace to broken human hearts. They had witnessed some of the greatest advances in human history (made by the Babylonians, the Greeks, and the Romans), yet their everyday lives still seemed meaningless and empty. They were trapped under the iron fist of Rome, a ruthless enemy who didn't believe in their God. And so the first century Jews became convinced that if they could just get a new king, a king who believed in the God of Israel, everything would get better. All they needed was a king who would punish Rome and restore Israel to her rightful place as God's Kingdom here on earth. In human terms it makes sense, doesn't it? We usually look for physical answers to our spiritual problems. But Jesus came with a very different message—a message that included the cure. But in order to embrace this cure we have to first understand the nature of our disease.

THE BEATITUDES

In Matthew chapter 5, Jesus begins what is known as the Sermon on the Mount (which is, without a doubt, the greatest sermon ever given) with a group of sayings that have become known as the Beatitudes, a phrase that means "the Blessings." Throughout the remainder of this book we will carefully study our Lord's words, that include His cure for what ails the human heart. Jesus is going to teach us some unexpected and life-changing truths. For example, He will reveal to us that:

1) Often, the way *up* can only be found when we're willing to bow *down*.

2) We have to deal with our *sorrow* before we can find true *joy*.

3) We will probably have to endure *persecution*, if we want to experience God's power.

4) *Dying* to self is actually the way to feel the most *alive*.

When we finish this amazing section of Scripture, we'll see that Jesus wants us to understand an essential truth—because our problem isn't physical, the cure won't be physical either. Until we understand the depth and nature of our disease, we will never understand the nature of the cure. It wasn't a new king the people of Israel needed in order to get right with God. It was a new understanding of their brokenness and sin, that separated them from their Heavenly Father. They felt empty and alone because they were not in proper relationship to the One who had created them.

What they needed most of all was the humility to recognize their sin and to accept God's grace (instead of their own efforts) as the solution to overcoming their problems. As much as I might want to see a change in the leadership of my country, true spiritual revival won't come from our political leaders. As much as I would love to see science solve all of our medical problems, true health won't come from research. As much as I would love to see every child receive a great education, true knowledge and wisdom won't come from our schools.

As we will learn from the words of Jesus in Matthew chapter 5, transformation must start in the hearts of God's people—a people who humbly bow down and receive God's grace; a people who surrender control and stop trying to be God; a people who are willing to accept what God has to offer. Only then will we find healing for our broken hearts, forgiveness to bind up our wounds, and unrelenting love to give our lives meaning and purpose.

Jesus describes the people who are transformed by God in this manner as salt and light. "You are the salt of the earth . . . You are the light of the world. A city on a hill cannot be hidden. Neither do people light a lamp and put it under a bowl. Instead they put it on its stand, and it gives light to everyone in the house. In the same way, let your light shine before men, that they may see your good deeds and praise your Father in heaven" (Matt. 5:13a, 14–16).

Salt cures, and light reveals the truth. If we are willing to face our sickness and receive God's cure, not only will we be made whole, but we will also be given the privilege of shining the light of God's truth into the lives of others, so they too can find the cure!

GOING DEEPER

1) Reread Psalm 14:1–3. What do you think of when you read these words?

2) Is it possible to believe in God and still deny Him, by the way we live?

3) Do you know anyone who as survived a bout of cancer? How did hearing the diagnosis change their life?

4) Are you ready to accept your spiritual diagnosis?

CHAPTER 2

WHATEVER IT TAKES

Blessed are the poor in spirit, for theirs is the kingdom of heaven.

Matthew 5:3

THE SETTING

TWO THOUSAND YEARS AGO, JESUS was born into a culture that was every bit as broken as the one we live in today. The nation of Israel was subject to the rule of Rome, a brutal empire that dominated the Mediterranean world. Because the Jewish people had rejected God and had lived in apostasy for over four hundred years, Israel had been reduced to a mere shadow of the glory it had enjoyed when its leaders walked closely with God. Men like David and Solomon were not perfect, but their lives were characterized by an intimate knowledge of their Creator. This knowledge fueled a love relationship with God, which enabled these great leaders to guide Israel through a time of unparalleled affluence. But by the time of Jesus' birth, the religious leaders had lost their way. Instead of seeking intimacy with God, they focused on empty religious rituals. Holiness was determined by how closely you followed the letter of the Law, instead of how closely you walked with God. The Pharisees and Sadducees spent most of their time arguing over minute details in the Torah, looking for new rules and regulations to follow, instead of offering hope to the desperate masses buried under the weight of Roman occupation.

Because of these conditions, the daily lives of the Jewish people were filled with drudgery and hardship. The Roman overlords took the best of everything the Jews worked so hard to produce. Their once great religion had been stripped of its ability to offer any hope. This was an atmosphere ripe for rebellion and war. If ever there was time for a dynamic leader to step up and take advantage of this dissatisfaction, this was the time. The people were desperate for freedom from Rome and hope for the future!

Into this chaos stepped a charismatic young rabbi with an un-expected message—a message that offered both freedom and hope, but not in the way the people were expecting. While the masses were focused on their external circumstances, Jesus was focused on the interior of their hearts. And it is here, at this point of contention, that Jesus chose to share some of the most powerful words ever spo-ken, words that hold the cure for what ails the sinful human heart.

"Now when he saw the crowds, he went up on a mountainside and sat down. His disciples came to him, ²and he began to teach them, saying: ³'Blessed are the poor in spirit, for theirs is the king-dom of heaven'" (Matt. 5:1–3).

I want you to try and imagine this scene as it was unfolding. When we look at the end of Matthew chapter 4, we see that Jesus had begun His ministry in Galilee by demonstrating God's ability to meet the people's needs.

> Jesus went throughout Galilee, teaching in their synagogues, preaching the good news of the kingdom, and healing every disease and sickness among the people. [24]News about him spread all over Syria, and people brought to him all who were ill with various diseases, those suffering severe pain, the demon-possessed, those having seizures, and the paralyzed, and he healed them. [25]Large crowds from Galilee, the Decapolis, Jerusalem, Judea and the region across the Jordan followed him. – Matt. 4:23–25

As Jesus began to demonstrate God's mercy and grace by healing the sick and delivering those who were demon-possessed, He became what we would call, in today's vernacular, a "celebrity". As a result of His fame, large crowds wanted to be near Him.

But instead of soaking in their praise and encouraging their adulation, Jesus took His disciples and retreated from the crowd. What could have been His motivation for doing this? Wasn't His goal to reach the lost? I believe the answer is very simple. The crowd's motivation for following Jesus was wrong. It wasn't because they were grateful for what God had done on their behalf. It wasn't because they were overwhelmed by His display of mercy and grace. It wasn't because they desired a personal relationship with God. And it certainly wasn't because they now had a passionate desire to serve God and His Kingdom. The bottom line was they wanted Jesus to take care of them and make their lives better. They were anticipating a Messiah who would come and throw off the shackles of Rome. By performing signs and wonders in their midst, they assumed that Jesus must be the long-awaited (physical) Savior of the (physical) Jewish nation. You can imagine what they were thinking after they watched Jesus perform His miracles: "Hey, if this guy can heal the sick, cast out demons, and provide food for the hungry, then surely He can destroy the Roman armies and restore Israel to her rightful place. If we just stay close to this guy, He'll take care of everything."

But this takes us back to what we said in the last chapter. If you don't understand the nature of your disease, you won't understand how to find the cure. Their problem wasn't Rome; it was the denial of their need for God. Their problem wasn't external, it was internal. It was the condition of their hearts. And so Jesus came to set them free, not from the tyranny of Rome, but from the tyranny of self, from the constant pull of selfishness and pride.

SOME THINGS NEVER CHANGE

This misunderstanding of the nature of the problem is not unique to the Jewish people of Jesus' day. We are also too often focused on the wrong things. A good example of this is when we judge a person's success based solely on his or her level of achievement. And sadly, this is true even in Christian circles. But God doesn't look at outward appearances, He looks at the heart. God is more interested in what you are becoming on the inside, than what you show the world on the outside. And this is where we so often get it wrong. Let me give you an example. What if I, as the pastor of a church, could stand up and deliver an inspiring message every week: a message that challenged my congregation to grow? What if I could also do a fantastic job of officiating great weddings and funeral services, organize ministry outreach to our community, and as a result of all of this activity, our church grew in numbers and financial stability? If all of this went on for several years, would that make me successful? Before you answer that question, let me add some additional information. What if you found out that, during my spare time, I was cheating on my wife, I was spending several hours every week looking at pornography on my computer, I was lying on my taxes to the IRS, and I was stealing small amounts of money from the church for my own personal gain? Now remember, the church continued to grow. Would I still be successful? Of course not!

What I am, and what I am becoming on the inside, is more important than what I do on the outside. Jesus addresses this in Matthew 7: "Watch out for false prophets. They come to you in sheep's clothing, but inwardly they are ferocious wolves. [16] By their fruit you will recognize them. Do people pick grapes from thorn bushes, or figs from thistles? [17] Likewise every good tree bears good fruit, but a bad tree bears bad fruit" (Matt. 7:15–17). You can only fool people for so long. At some point your outer actions will be affected by your inner life. We see this over and over, when people in prominent positions of leadership (both inside and outside the church) try to live one way in public and another way in private. But this never works. Jim Bakker, Jimmy Swaggart, Bill Clinton, Eliot Spitzer, Tiger Woods, Kobe Bryant, and Marv Albert are all examples of this, and the list goes on and on. And so Jesus says, "Stop kidding yourself; instead of focusing on outward appearances while selfishness and pride fill your heart, focus instead on surrendering your heart to me. Only I can help you become the person God created you to be."

Returning to Matthew 5, we begin to understand why Jesus left the adoring crowd and went up on the mountainside to spend time teaching His disciples, "Now when he saw the crowds, he went up on a mountainside and sat down. His disciples came to him" (Matt. 5:1). Like the crowd, His disciples were looking for the wrong things from Jesus. They too wanted Jesus to rise up as Messiah and destroy Rome so they could be free. These young men were fired up and ready to do whatever Jesus said. If there was going to be a new kingdom set up in their generation, they wanted to be part of it. Whatever it would take, they would be ready! With great anticipation they hung on His every word! And so His first sentence must have stunned them into silence—"Blessed are the poor in spirit, for theirs is the kingdom of heaven" (Matt. 5:3). What in the world is Jesus talking about? Blessed are the poor in spirit? Isn't it the person full of self-confidence, the person with great ideas and inspirations, the person fueled by huge ambitions, the one who gets the praise of men—isn't that the person who is truly blessed?

Like so much else that Jesus taught, this runs absolutely counter to everything we hear in our culture. And certainly, by what we see in the Gospel accounts about His disciples, it was counter to what they thought as well. Many times during Jesus' ministry, while He was focused on the inward change necessary for broken individuals to find wholeness, His disciples were busy arguing about which one of them would be the greatest in Jesus' new kingdom. We find a perfect example in Luke 9. "An argument started among the disciples as to which of them would be the greatest. [47]Jesus, knowing their thoughts, took a little child and had him stand beside him. [48]Then he said to them, 'Whoever welcomes this little child in my name welcomes me; and whoever welcomes me welcomes the one who sent me. For he who is least among you all—he is the greatest'" (Luke 9:46–48). Jesus obviously had a very different idea than His disciples as to what constitutes greatness. And because of this difference, being poor in spirit was not a characteristic that His followers seemed to value. It's very much the same for us in our culture. We are raised to believe that everything revolves around us and our personal desires. We're inundated by television commercials that are designed to foster this belief. Whatever I think I want, I should be able to have, and when this happens, then I will be happy. "If I get the right haircut, the right car, the best house, etc., then I'll be satisfied!"

I'LL NEVER ASK FOR ANYTHING AGAIN

When my son Nathan was about fifteen years old, he became interested in playing the drums. Of course his first thought was that he needed an expensive set to practice on. Thinking this was a fad, we bought him a cheap drum set for Christmas and told him that if he practiced hard and saved his money, we'd go halves with him on the expensive set the following year. Much to our surprise, Nathan kept up his end of the deal, practicing for hours each day and saving money from his dishwashing job to pay his half. After he and I loaded the new drums in our van, Nathan looked at me and said, "Thank you so much, I'll never ask for anything else again!" And I'm convinced that in that moment, he really believed that statement to be true! But of course, as we all find out in life, the drums weren't enough to satisfy all of Nathan's wants and desires. And as you can probably guess, since that time, he has asked for other things.

We are so thoroughly and deeply conditioned by our culture to think that the world revolves around us, that connecting the idea of being poor in spirit to blessings and success isn't even on our radar. This leads us back to our text and a very important question: what exactly does Jesus mean when He says, "Blessed are the poor in spirit, for theirs is the Kingdom of Heaven"? I agree with Christian author and speaker W. Phillip Keller, that the key to understanding our Lord's words here is to make sure we understand what He means by the word *spirit*. According to Keller:

> In our contemporary, non-Christian society, man is considered to be a dual being. He is said to have a body with its physical drives, desires and daily habits. He is also said to have a personality . . . or, as some put it, "person." This personality is made up of his mind with its thought processes, his emotions with all of their feelings and sensations, and his volition, or will, with which decisions are made and aims maintained.[1]

According to the modern secular view, each individual is the one in sole control of his or her life, through the decisions they make. At the core of this view is the belief that evolution is the sole driving force of life.

But the Bible gives us a very different picture. It reveals to us that man is actually made up of three parts, not two. According to Keller, "God's revelation is that man is in fact a tripartite being. He does have a body with all its physical capabilities. He does have a person with all of its soulish capabilities of thought, emotion and

---

1   W. Phillip Keller, *Salt for Society* (Waco, TX: Word, 1981), 25–26.

volition. But beyond this he also possesses a spirit with its capacity to know God who is Spirit; to see and understand God in a clear conscience; to have intimate and personal communion with God in spirit and truth."[2]

COMMUNION WITH GOD

Keller's point is an important one for us to remember: of all God's creatures, only human beings have this spiritual capability to see and understand God. We alone have the privilege of intimate and personal communion with the God who is Spirit. Jesus refers to this in John 4: "God is spirit, and his worshipers must worship in the Spirit and in truth" (John 4:24). An inability to understand the central role that the human spirit plays in our capacity to have a relationship with God is a major stumbling block for many people. Again, we return to Keller's analysis, "In our society, in our education, in our science we have been taught that we can function without spiritual reference to God. In our pride and humanistic arrogance we have been led to believe that we can get along readily without Him. He is totally ignored, bypassed and treated as if of no consequence."[3] As argued by atheists and humanistic leaders, belief in God is "the opiate of the masses,"[4] "a crutch for weak minds."[5]

But here in our text, Jesus makes it clear that the exact opposite is true. It is only after God's Spirit breathes life into our spirits that we are even able to experience spiritual life. According to the apostle Paul, until this new spiritual birth takes place we have no ability

---

2   Ibid., 26.
3   Ibid.
4   Karl Marx, http://www.allthelikes.com/quotes.php?quoteId=1839615&app=16045 5259901.
5   Jesse Ventura, http://www.ffxiah.com/forum/topic/9538/jesse-venturas-comments-on-religion/.

to understand the things of God: "The man without the Spirit does not accept the things that come from the Spirit of God, for they are foolishness to him, and he cannot understand them, because they are spiritually discerned" (1 Cor. 2:14). And this brings us back to our text in Matthew. Until we recognize the poverty and brokenness of our spirits apart from God's help, there is no possibility of coming to know God. Let me repeat that: until we recognize the poverty and brokenness of our spirits apart from God's help, there is no possibility of coming to know God.

It is human pride, arrogance, and self-assurance that lead individuals to believe they have no need for God. This has been the issue between God and man since the fall in the Garden of Eden. Adam and Eve believed the lie that they didn't need God. This sinful desire to put ourselves in the place of God is at the center of every struggle we face as human beings. And this is why Jesus started at this point in His description of the cure. *Please listen to me on this point.* If you don't sense, deep within your spirit, a recognition of your need for God; if you do not feel the brokenness of your spiritual condition apart from God; if there is no longing for things to be made right in your heart and life; then there is little or no chance you will experience the blessing that Jesus promises to all who are poor in spirit. This takes us back to our opening chapter: you have to recognize your illness before you will accept the cure. You need to be made aware of your terminal condition before you're ready to say, "whatever it takes, God, I'm ready!"

One of the best illustrations of this in Scripture comes from Matthew chapter 9: "Just then a woman who had been subject to bleeding for twelve years came up behind him and touched the edge of his cloak. ²¹She said to herself, 'If I only touch his cloak, I will be healed.' ²²Jesus turned and saw her. 'Take heart, daughter,' he said, 'your faith has healed you.' And the woman was healed from that moment" (Matt. 9:20–22). After twelve years of sickness and pain, this woman recognized that she could not take care of her problem on her own. Her only hope for a cure was Jesus. And whether we are puffed up with arrogance and pride, or broken and hopeless like this woman, God's gracious and generous Spirit does not leave us alone in our helplessness. He pursues us, He draws us to Himself, and He even causes us to seek and search for Him. Once our eyes are opened to His glory and grace, we begin to recognize our true condition: "Forgive me Lord, for I am a sinner!" "Yes Lord, I am poor in spirit." "I am empty, apart from You." "I need your saving grace and renewing Spirit."

And here is where the unexpected takes place. When we reach this point, we are truly blessed! It is at this point that we become children of God. In the words of the apostle John, "Yet to all who received him, to those who believed in his name, he gave the right to become children of God— ¹³children born not of natural descent, nor of human decision or a husband's will, but born of God" (John 1:12–13). It's at this point that we receive the infilling of His Spirit, giving us a brand new life: a life in which God's Spirit begins to heal the wounds of the past; a life in which His love begins to mend our broken hearts; and a life in which His presence begins to fill the empty void that in the past has stripped our lives of hope. When our Lord says, "Blessed are the poor in spirit, for theirs is the kingdom of heaven," He is promising us that when we reach this point (the point where we recognize our true spiritual condition and accept

God's offer of new spiritual life through our Savior)—this is the point at which we inherit the Kingdom of Heaven.

The Kingdom of Heaven is not the establishment of some earthly kingdom, as the disciples were hoping. It is instead the establishment of God's government in the heart of every believer. It signifies the surrender of our hearts, minds, and souls to the Lordship of our Savior Jesus Christ. Remember, Jesus said that "the kingdom of God is within you" (Luke 17:21). In essence, this means surrendering control of our lives to the Spirit of God as He dwells in our hearts. The Kingdom of God is any place, including the human heart, where God's will is recognized as sovereign.

When we become poor in spirit, we willingly surrender control of our hearts to the direction of the Holy Spirit. We give up self-control and selfish ambition in exchange for God's will for our lives. Like our Lord on the night He was betrayed, the cry of our hearts becomes, "Not my will, but yours be done." Above all else, we will desire to do God's will and work, regardless of the cost. We can actually say with sincerity, "Whatever it takes, God, I'm ready!" Like a cancer patient who will submit his body to the doctor's knife in order to get rid of that part of himself that is riddled with disease, a person who is poor in spirit willingly submits himself to the truth of God's Word; a truth that cuts like a knife at the sin and selfishness that riddles the human heart.

GOING DEEPER

1) When I look at my relationship with God, am I willing to admit that I bring nothing to the table?

2) Am I willing to admit that I need God's help every day of my life?

3) Have I surrendered my will to God, or am I still trying to control everything in my life, including my relationship with Jesus?

4) Have I ever experienced what it means to be poor in spirit?

If you can answer "yes" to one or more of these questions, you heart is being prepared to hear our Lord's words in the next chapter.

CHAPTER 3

JOY COMES IN THE MOURNING

Blessed are those who mourn, for they will be comforted.

Matthew 5:4

A FUNERAL FOR A FRIEND

BELIEVE IT OR NOT, ONE of the highlights of my Christian life was attending the funeral of an African-American friend named Julia. Before I became a pastor, I was a financial planner, and Julia was one of my clients. She had a deep faith in Jesus Christ, which was reflected in every area of her life. I loved meeting with Julia, because we talked more about Jesus than we ever did about money and finances. Over the last six months of her battle with cancer, I had the privilege of meeting and praying with her several times. I was a new Christian and I had never seen this type of faith before. Nothing that the doctors or the disease threw at her seemed to shake her faith in God. Most of the time, Julia was the one doing the encouraging! After she died, I was invited to her funeral, and was honored to attend. I was the only Caucasian in a very large

African-American church, and yet I never once felt out of place. As the service began, I experienced a peace and joy that is almost indescribable. For almost two hours, I sat there as her friends and family celebrated both her life and her faith in God. I walked into that funeral with a heavy heart of sorrow and grief, but I walked out of that funeral with an unspeakable joy. On the way home I was overwhelmed by a sense of the goodness and the grace of God! When I look back on that moment of time, I can't help but think about what Jesus said, "Blessed are those who mourn, for they will be comforted" (Matt. 5:4).

Although it goes against everything we try to convince ourselves of, as human beings we actually need times of mourning in our lives. In order to truly appreciate all that we have been given in this life by God, we actually need times of loss and pain, times when we wonder how we're going to be able to hang on. It is these deep feelings of sorrow which lead to mourning, that force us to get serious about the situation we're facing. When we mourn, it reveals that we honestly and truly care in a deep way. Let me give you a couple of illustrations.

WHAT'S REALLY IMPORTANT

I remember watching a Detroit Lions football game when one of their offensive linemen got hurt. A hush fell over the crowd when it became obvious that he wasn't moving, and likely had no feeling in his body. Suddenly, thousands of people realized that the person they were watching being attended to by medical personnel might very well be paralyzed for the rest of his life. Something changed as he was wheeled out on a cart with his head fastened down so his neck wouldn't move. All of a sudden, the outcome of the game didn't seem that important.

Here's another example. Which is more meaningful: if someone comes to a party celebrating your recent promotion at work, or if they show up at a gathering to help comfort you because you're grieving the loss of a close family member? Although professional advancement is exciting and provides a great opportunity to celebrate with your close friends, it is during times of painful loss that you really discover those on whom you can depend.

There's something about the mourning process that cuts through the trivial things of life and focuses our hearts and minds on what is really important. Although my friend Julia suffered physically in her final days, she soared in her spirit as she turned to God for strength. The way she found such deep comfort in Christ under such painful circumstances was a profound reminder to those of us who knew her, that, no matter how difficult our physical circumstances might be, they don't change God's ability to keep His promises to His children. Promises like these:

> Never will I leave you; never will I forsake you.
> – Heb. 13:5

> He gives strength to the weary and increases the power of the weak. [30] Even youths grow tired and weary, and young men stumble and fall; [31] but those who hope in the LORD will renew their strength. They will soar on wings like eagles; they will run and not grow weary, they will walk and not be faint. – Isa. 40:29–31

Sometimes it is when we are the most weary, the most tired, and the most heartbroken that God becomes the most real! And as hard as it is for those of us who are obsessed with personal comfort to comprehend, at Julia's funeral it was the painful loss of a beloved sister in Christ that provided the opportunity to experience God's faithfulness in such a meaningful way. It was literally as we mourned our loss, that we began to experience God's blessings in a deeper way. And this leads us back to one of the most profound and important paradoxes in the Bible. It is when we mourn and face death that we find the true blessings and joy of life.

I DON'T WANT TO THINK ABOUT IT!

But in our contemporary culture, death, mourning, and all the grief that surrounds the end of life are subjects we try desperately to ignore. We would rather push them aside, change the subject, or not think about them at all. But when you look at the Gospels, you see that Jesus not only thought about these subjects, He often talked about them as well. In Matthew 5:4, He even went so far as to say that a person who mourns is blessed! "Blessed are those who mourn, for they will be comforted." Think about the significance of this principle. As Phillip Keeler observes, "Somehow He (Jesus) was sure that anyone who mourns is the recipient of a special and unusual benefit from above. In fact, He went even further to state that this individual, if indeed a follower of Christ, would experience comfort."[6]

The Greek word translated as *mourn* in this verse means to have a broken heart and a helpless, almost desperate, sorrow. It is not

---

6   Keller, *Salt* (Waco, TX: Word, 1981), 32.

simply being sad because things didn't go your way, or because someone else got more than you. It is instead a deep brokenness of spirit about a situation over which you realize you have no further control. "I can't make this better! I can't fix this situation!" There are at least three distinct ways in which a believer experiences this type of mourning, giving him an opportunity to experience the comfort Jesus promises: 1) physical death, 2) spiritual death, and 3) suffering on behalf of others. We'll address these in order.

PHYSICAL DEATH

As we saw in Julia's story, for the Christian, death is not something we have to fear. Instead, it opens a door for us to step into the personal presence of our Savior and Lord! It ushers us into a new life of intimacy with God that the Bible says is beyond our limited human ability to understand. Listen to what the Scriptures say awaits believers after physical death:

> But as it is written: "Eye has not seen, nor ear heard, nor have entered into the heart of man the things which God has prepared for those who love Him." – 1 Cor. 2:9 NKJV

> Do not let your hearts be troubled. Trust in God; trust also in me. [2] In my Father's house are many rooms; if it were not so, I would have told you. I am going there to prepare a place for you. [3]And if I go and prepare a place for you, I will come back and take you to be with me that you also may be where I am. – John 14:1–3

These are promises that are almost too wonderful to believe. But when you go through the mourning process as a Christian, and when you have an experience like I had at Julia's funeral, where God is so close, so personal, and so alive, these promises become real! And it is the living reality of these promises which gives those of us left behind the peace and strength we need to heal and move on. "Blessed are those who mourn, for they will be comforted." So certainly one way we are blessed and comforted in mourning is to be reminded and assured that physical death has no power over us because we have been given eternal life in Christ.

SPIRITUAL DEATH

Now beyond dealing with physical death, it is pretty clear from the text that Jesus was also talking about spiritual death. Like physical death, this is a subject many people don't care to talk about. I believe the primary reason is because there is so much misunderstanding in this area. According to Keller, "The Bible is very clear what spiritual death entails. Spiritual death means to be separated, cut off from God our Father. It is to be in that condition where there really is no correspondence between Him and us. It is to be alive physically and morally, yet unaware of His presence and power which impart a new dimension of life to us in the realm of our spirits."[7] Paul describes this spiritual death in the book of Ephesians:

> As for you, you were dead in your transgressions and sins, [2]in which you used to live when you followed the ways of this world and of the ruler of the kingdom of the air, the spirit who is now at work in those who are disobedient. [3]All of us also lived among them at one time, gratifying the cravings of our sinful nature

---

7   Ibid., 33.

and following its desires and thoughts. Like the rest, we were by nature objects of wrath. ⁴But because of his great love for us, God, who is rich in mercy, ⁵made us alive with Christ even when we were dead in transgressions—it is by grace you have been saved.
  – Eph. 2:1–5

Through this text we learn that God's love and faithfulness are the sources of spiritual life and communion with Christ. In other words, it is God's Spirit who breathes life into our spirits, bringing them from death to life. This is further supported in Colossians: "When you were dead in your sins and in the uncircumcision of your sinful nature, God made you alive with Christ. He forgave us all our sins, ¹⁴having canceled the written code, with its regulations, that was against us and that stood opposed to us; he took it away, nailing it to the cross" (Col. 2:13–14).

It is God who makes us alive by bringing us from spiritual death into new spiritual life. This is what Jesus means in John 3 when He says we must be born again to see the Kingdom of Heaven. However, this transformation can only take place when there is first a deep sense of mourning within the human heart over its condition of spiritual death. Again Keller gives us great insight into how this happens: "It is God's Spirit who comes to us, touching us in our spirits, convicting us that somehow there is a dimension in our lives where we are simply not alive. With a deep disquiet we sense that we are not in active communion with our Creator. There is something amiss."⁸

---

8   Ibid.

At this point we begin to experience an ache for a life that seems to be beyond the physical life we live every day. We sense that we are not in an authentic relationship with our Creator. There is something missing at the very core of our being. We are separated from God by our own unbelief, which, if not addressed, has the potential to become outright animosity and alienation. If we are truly seeking God, this ache and longing in our hearts will become a turning point in our lives. We will begin to recognize that we have no ability to change this condition in our own strength. Our longing will become despair over our sinful condition. And at this juncture, God's Spirit will begin showing us that something has to be made right between Him and us. Seeing ourselves for who we really are, we will confess our dead and lost condition, and begin to mourn our emptiness apart from God.

We see this in the sinner (described as a tax collector) who is desperately praying in Luke 18. "But the tax collector stood at a distance. He would not even look up to heaven, but beat his breast and said, 'God, have mercy on me, a sinner'" (Luke 18:13). Amazingly, it is at this point of mourning and brokenness that Jesus says we are blessed. In verse 14, Jesus goes on to say this about the tax collector who mourned his sin, "I tell you that this man, rather than the other, went home justified before God. For everyone who exalts himself will be humbled, and he who humbles himself will be exalted."

Remember what we said earlier, to *mourn* means to have a broken heart and a helpless, almost desperate, sorrow. It's not simply being sorry because you did something wrong and you got caught.

It's having a deep sorrow for your sins. Let me give you a humorous illustration. After staying at a hotel, a well-known businessman complained to the management about the bugs he had had in his room. Shortly thereafter, he received a letter from the hotel chain apologizing for any inconvenience he had experienced during his stay and assuring him that they take the cleanliness of their hotel rooms very seriously. The letter went on to explain that any time there was a complaint, the hotel staff would act immediately to eliminate the problem. They ended the letter by asking him to accept their deepest apologies and gave an assurance that they would use whatever resources were necessary to remedy the situation. However, when he got to the end of the letter, there was a sticky note attached to it, that someone had forgotten to remove before mailing the letter. The sticky note read, "Send this guy the bug note and if he continues to complain, offer him a free night."

Paul reminds us, "Godly sorrow brings repentance that leads to salvation and leaves no regret, but worldly sorrow brings death" (2 Cor. 7:10). It is godly sorrow over sin that brings about repentance, repentance then leads to forgiveness, and forgiveness leads to deliverance. In this Beatitude, Jesus is saying that there can be no true joy and no experience of the deeply comforting satisfaction which comes from being blessed, unless there is an honest sorrow for your sin. It is to the person who recognizes and admits their sinful condition that God's Spirit speaks comfort and consolation: "You are forgiven, you are cleansed, you are justified, you are set free from your sins, and you are accepted into the family of God." And even more amazingly, God doesn't stop there. He not only makes us alive spiritually, but He goes on to share our lives with us, as a constant companion and counselor. He assures us at every bump and bend in the road that we will always have the comfort of His companionship. I can't help but think back to when this truth became a reality in my life. I was living so far from God, caught up in everything the world says brings happiness and joy, and yet I could not extinguish the ache in my heart. But when I finally acknowledged my condition, mourning over the emptiness of my heart and life, Jesus' words became a reality in my heart: "Blessed are those who mourn, for they will be comforted." Just remembering the joy and peace and freedom that swept over me still gives me goose bumps today. God keeps His promises! He will give us new life, but first we must mourn our spiritual death.

SUFFERING WITH OTHERS

There is a third and final type of mourning that leads to God's comfort, which has to do with living as a Christian in a fallen world, living as people who have been given a new spiritual life through Christ. As a direct result of this new life, we should be very sensitive to the grief and suffering that is all around us. Our society is sick with a terminal illness that is destroying our families and friends. Only the believer delivered from death to life can appreciate the danger that surrounds him , and can thus carry a message of hope to those lost in the struggle. But sadly, there are many who profess to be Christians who yet feel a total indifference to the dead and dying all around them. There is an old saying that carries a lot of truth, "The dead do not mourn the dead." It is the ones alive to the pain of death who cry and weep for the loved ones they have lost. It is the living who cry out to God for the resurrection of the dead.

As Christians who understand the horrific consequences of spiritual death, we should experience the same intensity of mourning for the people we know who are living in rebellion against God. Jesus is making it clear that we are responsible to those lost people who God brings into our lives. Your salvation is not for you alone. Not only are we to mourn for our own sin, but also for the sin and brokenness of the culture we live in.

When was the last time you wept for someone lost in sin? Does your spirit ever cry out with sorrow for a society that is so broken and out of control? I am well aware that getting involved in the lives of others can be difficult. When we get our hands dirty helping others, the result can be personal pain. But Jesus says that when we truly mourn for those who are lost, we are blessed! And wrapped up in that blessing is the promise that we will receive God's special comfort. When we move out into the world looking for ways to represent Christ to the people we encounter, God's Spirit empowers us to overcome our own weaknesses, so we become vessels He can use to bring His healing power to bear on the situation! Paul describes this process for us: "For we are God's workmanship, created in Christ Jesus to do good works, which God prepared in advance for us to do" (Eph. 2:10).

GOING DEEPER

Jesus describes a whole new life waiting for those who accept their sinful condition, who mourn over their sin, and who allow God's Spirit to rule and reign in their hearts! I want you to ask yourself a couple of questions as we close this chapter:

1) Do you recognize your need?

2) Are you ready to get well?

Only Jesus offers healing and hope. If you are poor in spirit, and if you are ready to mourn, then you are well on your way to discovering a new life in Christ!

CHAPTER 4

POWER UNDER CONTROL

Blessed are the meek, for they will inherit the earth.

Matthew 5:5

MEEK OR WEAK?

LIKE THE FIRST TWO BEATITUDES, Jesus' words in verse 5 are clearly designed to challenge conventional wisdom. "Blessed are the meek, for they will inherit the earth" (Matt. 5:5). If you are like me, when you read this text your first thought is, "What in the world is He talking about here? Since when is a meek person blessed?" Isn't it the meek kid who gets pushed around at school? Isn't it the meek woman who finds herself sitting alone at parties? Isn't it the meek man who gets stuck with all the worst assignments at the office? This is a prime example of where the translation of Jesus' words from Greek to English leaves us at a great disadvantage. In order to fully understand the depth of what Jesus is saying in this text, we have to recapture the original meaning of the word *meek*. Certainly, in our culture today, this word does not have a positive connotation. According to Pastor Ray Pritchard, "It suggests many things, none of which are very appealing. If you tell someone you think they are meek, they probably won't take it as a compliment. In fact, they'll probably assume you are saying something negative about their character."[9]

I believe he is absolutely correct in his assessment. All you have to do is open a thesaurus and look up the word *meek*, and you will see why we hold it in such low esteem. If you do, you'll see words like humble, timid, submissive, gentle, docile, modest, compliant, and mild. Not exactly a blockbuster list of power words. And this illustrates our problem in trying to grasp Jesus' meaning. Try re-wording this Beatitude, using some of those words as a substitute for meek. *"Blessed are the timid, for they will inherit the earth."* It doesn't sound right, does it? How about, *"Blessed are the docile"?* Nothing about this statement points one in the direction of blessings.

I think if we are honest, most of us read this text and confuse the word *meek* with the word *weak*. And if that's the case, it's no wonder we don't want to be called meek. However, because Jesus said that meekness would be a characteristic found in His followers, we need to take the time to understand what He meant.

Author Philip Keller gives us some helpful insight through his childhood experience of growing up on a ranch in eastern Africa. One of his favorite times of year was when his dad would buy the oxen that were necessary for large-scale farming, before tractors were available. These large animals, called Brahma bulls, would arrive as wild animals, fighting and kicking and struggling

---

9   Ray Pritchard, in his sermon "The Right Stuff", January 1996, http://www.keepbe-lieving.com/sermon/1996-01-21-The-Right-Stuff/.

against the powerful restraints that were used to harness their great strength. Only after weeks of continual training, where the animals fought and kicked and struggled to the point of exhaustion, were these brute beasts finally tamed and ready to be trained for farming. But once they stopped fighting and began submitting themselves to the work they were bred to perform, the result was nothing short of miraculous. By harnessing the power of these large animals to pull plows, to rip out stumps, and to move large rocks, the farmers of East Africa were able to turn once barren and useless ground into productive and profitable farmland. Over the years, vast expanses of land were reclaimed, providing food to feed many thousands of hungry people. When left to their own wild nature, the power these oxen possessed made them dangerous and unpredictable. But once that power was under control and put to good use, their owners could feed and care for the oxen without any fear of personal harm.[10]

This story is a great illustration of what Jesus was describing when He used the word *meek* in Matthew 5:5. It is not by possessing immense strength and power that we achieve great things for God's Kingdom. It's only when our strength and power is brought under the control of our Heavenly Father that we become useful vessels for the work to which God has called us. In the original Greek, the word translated as *meek* carries the idea of power that could be harnessed for good. If you owned a meek horse, it was not a weak horse, but a powerful horse you were able to control. This has led many Bible scholars to define *meekness* as "power under control."

---

10   Keller, *Salt*, 40–42.

We find a similar Hebrew word used in Psalm 37 to describe a man who submits himself to the will of God:

> Be still before the LORD and wait patiently for him; do not fret when men succeed in their ways, when they carry out their wicked schemes. ⁸Refrain from anger and turn from wrath; do not fret—it leads only to evil. ⁹For evil men will be cut off, but those who hope in the LORD will inherit the land. ¹⁰A little while, and the wicked will be no more; though you look for them, they will not be found. ¹¹*But the meek will inherit the land and enjoy great peace.*
> – Ps. 37:7–11 (italics mine)

Once you contrast this powerful illustration of meekness with the prevailing view that it implies weakness, it becomes obvious that nothing could be further from the truth. In fact, in the book of Galatians, Paul describes meekness as a fruit of the Spirit: "But the fruit of the Spirit is love, joy, peace, longsuffering, gentleness, goodness, faith, meekness, temperance: against such there is no law" (Gal. 5:22–23 KJV). In Colossians he includes meekness as part of a Christians' daily attire: "Put on then, as God's chosen ones, holy and beloved, compassionate hearts, kindness, humility, meekness, and patience" (Col. 3:12 ESV). In fact, the deeper you dig into the usage of the word *meek* in the Scriptures, the more powerful its meaning becomes.

MEEKNESS IN ACTION

When we begin to see the importance God places on the characteristic of meekness throughout the Scriptures, it is interesting to note that only two people in the Bible are actually described using this word: Moses and Jesus. In the Old Testament book of Numbers, Moses was described as "very meek, more than all people who were on the face of the earth" (Num. 12:3 ESV). If you've had the chance to read Moses' life story, this is probably not the first word you would have come up with to describe the man God chose to lead the Israelites. After all, didn't Moses stare down Pharaoh, and demand that the most powerful ruler on earth release the Hebrew slaves? Later, with his people facing imminent destruction, didn't Moses hold out his staff and call upon God to part the Red Sea? And finally, when he was well over the age of eighty, wasn't it Moses who in anger struck a huge rock with his staff, causing water to flow in the desert for the thirsty Israelites? No, meekness would probably not even make the list of words you would think of to describe this man.

So what was it about Moses' character that caused God to label him as meek? When we take the time to study the section of Scripture where this statement is made, we not only find our answer, but also a wonderful example of what meekness looks like in action. In Numbers 12, a disagreement unfolds between Moses, his brother Aaron, and his sister Miriam. As is common in many families, the argument seems to start because Moses' brother and sister are not happy with the woman whom Moses has chosen as a wife. We pick up the story in verse 1: "Miriam and Aaron spoke against Moses because of the Cushite woman whom he had married, for he had married a Cushite woman. ²And they said, 'Has the LORD indeed spoken only through Moses? Has he not spoken through us also?' And the LORD heard it" (Num. 12:1–2 ESV). Notice that this text ends with the recognition that God heard Aaron and Miriam's criticism. The following is how Ray Pritchard describes God's response to this criticism:

> Numbers 12:1 tells us that Moses had married a Cushite woman (that is, a black African woman). His decision (which was not forbidden since God had not yet given the law) was criticized openly by his brother Aaron (the high priest) and Aaron's wife Miriam. "Has the Lord spoken only through Moses? Hasn't he also spoken through us?" (v.1) The answer, of course, is yes, God had spoken through them, but that didn't give them the right to criticize Moses. Verse 1 tells us that God "heard" their critical comments–a fact that does not bode well for them.
>
> Before we go on, please note that the criticism stems partly from the fact that Moses had entered into an interracial marriage. Though some commentators pass over this fact, the text explicitly says that it was Moses' marriage that caused the criticism. But Moses was not wrong to marry the Cushite woman providing she would join him in worshipping the God of Israel. While the Bible does forbid an "unequal yoke" of believer deliberately marrying an unbeliever (II Cor. 6:14–18), it does not forbid Christians to marry across racial or ethnic lines. For the Christian the issue is always the heart attitude toward Jesus Christ, not skin color or ethnic origin.
>
> So God calls Moses, Aaron and Miriam to meet him in front of the Tabernacle (another bad sign for the two offenders). Then he tells Aaron and Miriam to step forward

(trouble is on the way). Verses 6–8 record God's word to the two critics: "When a prophet of the Lord is among you, I reveal myself to him in visions, I speak to him in dreams. But this is not true of my servant Moses; he is faithful in all my house. With him I speak face to face, clearly and not in riddles; he sees the form of the Lord. Why then were you not afraid to speak against my servant Moses?" This is a devastating rebuke to Aaron and Miriam. "I speak to Moses face to face. He is my main man. I trust him with the future of my people. If I want to say anything about his wife, I'll do it myself. He doesn't need your criticism and I don't need your help. Who do you think you are to have any opinion at all about who Moses marries?" Ouch! The ax is about to fall. Verses 9–12 tell us the judgment. Miriam will be stricken with leprosy–the equivalent of AIDS in that generation. It is significant that Miriam now is white as snow from leprosy. It is as if God had said to her, "Moses' wife is black, and you think white is better. Fine, you're going to be white all over." It is a judgment fitted to the sin of racial prejudice. God despises the haughty attitude of those who look down on others simply because of the color of their skin. After all, man looks on the outside, but God judges the heart (I Sam. 16:7).[11]

Aaron's response to God's judgment is to make a complete about face. He admits the foolishness of his actions and pleads with Moses to intervene with God on Miriam's behalf. And here is where we

11   Pritchard, "The Right Stuff".

see what true meekness looks like in action. Instead of defending himself against the charges that his brother and sister have made against him, Moses stood mute and let God be his defender. When you look at the text, you can clearly see that Moses never spoke a word in his own defense; but he was quick to respond in Miriam's time of need. Moses' first words are recorded in verse 13 when he simply prays, "Please heal her, O God, I pray!"

How different might our lives be today, if you or I had responded to past criticisms with the same strength of character that Moses displayed with his siblings? How many needless arguments, broken friendships, and devastating family consequences could have been avoided, simply by developing a spirit of meekness?

Remember what I said earlier: meekness in no way implies weakness. I'm not suggesting that as Christians we need to become punching bags for others to knock around. Moses was not a doormat; consistently throughout the Scriptures we see him standing up for the things that really matter to God. But in this case, when it boils down to protecting himself from unwarranted personal attacks, Moses leaves that up to God. And here is where we find the real secret behind the power of meekness. Because Moses had surrendered his life to God's control, he knew that anything he was capable of doing in his own strength was insignificant, compared to what God was able and willing to do on his behalf.

At its core, meekness is the faith to believe that God always has my best interest at heart. I can trust God with the outcome of this event, *even and especially* when the outcome is not in my control. Now, as we go back and revisit our definition of meekness as "power under control", we can see the full spiritual ramifications.

If I say that I trust God and have placed my faith in Jesus Christ as my personal Savior, then it stands to reason that meekness—*faith to believe that God always has my best interest at heart*—should become evident in my daily life. The more I learn to trust God, the more of my own power and will I surrender to God. And the more of my own power and will I surrender to God, the more meekness—the more faith—I will begin to display in my actions.

I read a story recently that illustrates this point: A young man named Sam was going to be one of the first African exchange students to attend Taylor University, a private Christian school located in Upland, Indiana. When the young man arrived, he was treated to a tour of the campus by the president of the university. When the tour was completed, the president asked Sam where he would like to live. Sam's reply was immediate, "If there is a room that no one else wants, I'll live there." The president was forced to turn his head because of the tears that filled his eyes. He had previously welcomed thousands of students, none of whom had shown that kind of meekness and character.[12]

JESUS' EXAMPLE

A perfect illustration of this principle is found in Jesus' behavior on the night in which He was betrayed. As He faced the horror of death by crucifixion and the unspeakable pain of separation from His Heavenly Father, Jesus declared, "Father, if you are willing, take this cup from me; yet not my will, but yours be done" (Luke 22:42). Jesus understood that the fulfillment of God's redemptive

---

12   Bryan Wilkerson, in his sermon "In God We Trust (Though We'd Rather Pay Cash)", September   2008,   http://www.preachingtoday.com/illustrations/2008/september/4092908.html.

plan was the very purpose for which He came to earth. This meant that His short-term prospect of pain, as terrible as it was going to be, would lead to immeasurable eternal glory, both for himself and for His Heavenly Father. Jesus' meekness in the face of Roman crucifixion was the single most powerful act a human has ever accomplished. There is nothing weak about the godly characteristic of meekness.

This is why Jesus was able to accurately describe himself as meek in the Gospel of Matthew, "Come unto me, all ye that labour and are heavy laden, and I will give you rest. ²⁹Take my yoke upon you, and learn of me; for I am *meek* and lowly in heart: and ye shall find rest unto your souls. ³⁰For my yoke is easy, and my burden is light" (Matt. 11:28–30 KJV; italics mine). After demonstrating the power of meekness to overcome fear and doubt, Jesus now invites us to share in His victory as we surrender control of our lives to Him. The picture of taking up His yoke is that of two oxen pulling together to plow a field. In this illustration, Jesus promises that if we will place our lives in His yoke, trusting Him to pick the direction we need to go, He will do the majority of the pulling along the way.

SUPERNATURAL

This reminds us that the Christian life is supernatural in nature. You and I can never achieve meekness on our own. Jesus makes this clear when he says, "Nevertheless I tell you the truth. It is to your advantage that I go away; for if I do not go away, the Helper will not come to you; but if I depart, I will send Him to you" (John 16:7 NKJV). He is reminding us that one of the primary roles of the Holy Spirit is to take up residence in the heart of believers, providing the supernatural power we need to live a new life. When you and I finally reach this point in our Christian journey, the point where we willingly surrender control to our Lord, we exchange the shackles of self-control and the weight of failed expectations for the joy of the Holy Spirit's guidance and direction. What a deal! This is the beauty of meekness! When understood in this context, it is no wonder that Jesus describes the person who lives this way as blessed.

The idea that meekness leads to blessings was driven home to me in a powerful way recently when our church began hosting Celebrate Recovery meetings on Monday evenings. Celebrate Recovery is a Christ-centered twelve-step program started by Saddleback Church in the early 1990's. Along with the twelve steps used in a typical Alcoholics Anonymous meeting, Pastor Rick Warren and his staff designed their curriculum to include the biblical references for each step, along with an additional eight-step Road to Recovery (which just happens to be based on the Beatitudes). As people work through the steps, admitting that they are powerless in their own strength, recognizing they need God's grace and forgiveness, and surrendering control of their lives to the Lordship of Jesus Christ, something wonderful and life-changing takes place. A person who was formerly lost in the patterns of self-destructive behavior that led to addictions and bondage, instead begins to experience the freedom and blessings of a life directed by God.

ROSEMARY'S STORY

To further illustrate this point, let me share Rosemary's story with you. Rosemary began attending our church early in the spring of 2012. Within a few weeks of her first visit, she called me to ask if the attacks of anxiety and fear that she was experiencing meant that she was doing something wrong as a Christian. After meeting together and talking about the daily struggles she faced, I realized that Rosemary was carrying a load too great for anyone to carry on their own. As the primary caregiver to a dying mother, the wife of a long-haul truck driver who was on the road thirty days at a time, and a woman who fought a daily battle with depression and anxiety, she was sinking under the weight of so much responsibility. Shortly after our counseling sessions began, Rosemary's mother passed away. Without that familiar role as her mother's caregiver, which had served to keep her mind occupied and forced her to leave her house, Rosemary's first instinct was to isolate herself. As anyone who has ever dealt with depression, anxiety, or fear will confirm, isolation only serves to intensify the internal struggle that rages in the heart and mind. The loss of hope began to seem overwhelming.

But here is where Rosemary's story takes an amazing and wonderful turn. After allowing her anxiety to keep her away from Sunday morning services for fifteen straight weeks, somehow she found the courage to attend a Celebrate Recovery meeting. While sitting in a circle with other women, all of whom were honest enough to admit their personal struggles, Rosemary finally realized she was not alone. As she heard testimonies of God's work in breaking the chains of bondage and fear in the lives of other women, she began to believe that He could do the same thing for her. That next Sunday she fought her fear and came to church. She felt as if the message that day was written just for her. She also found the opportunity to use the gift of compassion (a gift that God had given her to take care of her mother) to come alongside an elderly woman in our church who needed help with her personal affairs. Today, although she still has times when she has feelings of anxiety and fear, Rosemary is experiencing victory. She consistently attends Sunday services, has joined a small group, regularly attends Celebrate Recovery, and never misses a chance to share her gift of compassion by making herself available to serve the needs of others in our church body.

When Jesus says, "Blessed are the meek, for they will inherit the earth" (Matt. 5:5), he ends this Beatitude with a promise. Not only will the meek experience blessings, but they will also receive the earth as their inheritance. Now I understand that Jesus is certainly referring to a time when He returns as King, and His people will rule and reign with Him on a new earth. But I believe Rosemary's story shows us how this promise is also for today. Her victory in Christ is a perfect example of how meekness (surrendering control to God) can literally open the door to experiencing a whole new life here on earth. Rosemary's world used to be confined to the spaces she felt she could control: her house, the inside of her car, and an occasional trip to the store. Today, because of the freedom and authority that she now experiences through her relationship with Jesus Christ, the whole earth is her inheritance.

GOING DEEPER

1) What areas of your life still need to be surrendered to Jesus Christ?

2) What comes to mind when you consider giving up control of your life to the Lord?

3) What is the first step you need to take in order to begin experiencing the blessings offered through this Beatitude?

CHAPTER 5

HUNGRY HEARTS

Blessed are those who hunger and thirst for righteousness,
for they will be filled.

Matthew 5:6

THE POWER OF HUNGER

EVERY JANUARY, MILLIONS OF AMERICANS and billions of people around the world stop everything else they are doing to sit down and watch the Super Bowl. Interestingly, over the last twenty years, much of the focus has shifted from the actual game to the television commercials. All of the anticipation and hype that used to be reserved for the action on the football field has slowly shifted to the competition between advertising campaigns. Everyone wonders, "Which new outlandish commercial will create the biggest stir?" Powerful corporations are willing to spend millions of dollars just to get their fifteen- or thirty-second shot at fame. Why are advertisers willing to pay so much money for such a short amount of time? The answer is quite simple—because it works. They know if they can get us to emotionally connect to their slogan and image, it will influence our choices of what we buy. In essence, they are buying real estate in our minds.

The advertising and marketing industry has figured out what Jesus knew over two thousand years ago: if you can successfully connect an image to an idea in a person's mind, you can influence the way they see the world. For example, what do you think of when you see two golden arches? How about a black swoosh? McDonald's and Nike have successfully inundated our minds with these images, and as a result we tend to favor their products when we feel hungry or need new running shoes. Pastor Ed Sasnett describes the process well: "Madison Avenue has two deliberate actions as a part of their strategy. First, they suggest our world is incomplete without their product. Second, they give us that image over and over. Nike knows we won't buy a pair of their sneakers after one commercial, but after a thousand the idea begins to influence our choices."[13] The longer we feel connected to the image, the more power it has to motivate and drive our actions. What used to be a casual "I want that" now becomes a driving ambition: "I must have that new Mercedes Benz, even if it means I work extra hours and sacrifice time with my family."

When you look at Jesus' teaching throughout the Gospels, you realize He understood this principle very well. Whether He was comparing the Kingdom of God to a mustard seed, a hunk of leaven, or a pearl, our Lord continually provided His followers with word pictures to help them remember the important truths He was teaching. Whenever His followers would encounter one of these

---

13   Ed Sasnet, in his sermon "Happy are the Starved", http://www.sermoncentral.com/sermons/happy-are-the-starved-ed-sasnett-sermon-on-character-93392.asp.

everyday objects, there would be a reinforcement of the message Jesus had taught. And this leads us to the fourth Beatitude, where Jesus uses two powerful images, hunger and thirst, to drive home His point. I can almost guarantee that, unless you are physically sick or in the middle of an intentional fast, you will act upon these two powerful motivators at some point today.

> Blessed are those who hunger and thirst for righteous-
> ness, for they will be filled. – Matt. 5:6

Clearly, Jesus is using an illustration of a physical truth we can all understand, in order to teach a much deeper spiritual reality. When we experience physical hunger or thirst, we will be driven by the desire to satisfy those cravings. In a very real sense, our appetite will control the actions we take. Everything else fades to the background and the focus becomes: "How can I obtain food and water?" In the same way our appetites control our physical lives, Jesus is teaching us that our appetites also drive our spiritual lives.

YOU ARE WHAT YOU EAT

The importance of this truth is emphasized in the popular saying, "you are what you eat." Now I know when some of you read those words, you winced at the thought of how poorly you have eaten lately. Looking around at the general physical health in our culture, particularly with fast food and unhealthy eating habits, very few people would argue that this principle is not true. In fact, nutritionists tell us there is a direct link between our appetites, our diets, and our health. Medical science has been able to demonstrate that too much salt or sugar in a person's diet harms the body. Eating only fatty foods can cause serious consequences to our cholesterol levels as well as the health of our hearts. This principle is so well established that whole industries have arisen, offering everything from advice to very costly products in an effort to help us live healthier lifestyles. In almost every case, the main objective of these programs is to help us learn to control or to retrain our appetites. In some cases better health requires that we stop eating or drinking certain products altogether. In other cases, improved health means retraining our appetites so that we start to desire foods and beverages we never considered in the past.

Hopefully at this point it is not a big leap for us to see the spiritual ramifications of this principle. Whatever direction our desires and appetites lead us is the direction our life is likely to go. Whatever you seek in life, you tend to find. For some of you, it may be a quest for sexual pleasure or financial independence or personal fame that fuels your daily activities. For others, it may be something nobler. Maybe you are looking for a great cause worth giving your life to. Regardless of what has motivated your daily activities up until this point, Jesus challenges us to reevaluate our spiritual appetites. "Blessed are those who hunger and thirst after righteousness, for they will be filled" (Matt. 5:6). As usual, Jesus cuts right to the heart of an essential spiritual truth: when it comes to your spiritual life, it is your hunger that ultimately determines your spiritual health.

WHAT DOES RIGHTEOUSNESS MEAN?

Now that we realize the power of hunger and thirst to drive our appetites, both physical and spiritual, it is important that we figure out what Jesus means when He tells us to "hunger and thirst after righteousness." What exactly is righteousness? This is a question that stumps many believers. We may have a vague idea that it involves godly behavior, but my guess is that few Christians could come up with a satisfactory definition off the top of their heads. Ray Pritchard points out a very important principle for us, "Whenever you come upon a term in the Bible you don't understand, it's always helpful to look at other passages of Scripture that may shed light on it."[14] Thankfully, we don't have to go very far to begin to find an answer. Just four verses later in Matthew 5, Jesus tells us something important about righteousness: "Blessed are those who are persecuted because of righteousness, for theirs is the kingdom of heaven" (Matt. 5:10). Based on the two examples of righteousness used in the Beatitudes, we can conclude that we are to hunger and thirst after a life that will lead others to persecute us because of our faith in Christ. When we begin to live a life that is righteous, we will be distinctive from the world. In simple terms, our genuine Christian faith will cause some to oppose us.

Our next text can also be found in Matthew 5, "For I tell you that unless your righteousness surpasses that of the Pharisees and the teachers of the law, you will certainly not enter the kingdom of heaven" (Matt. 5:20). This is a very important verse in helping us to understand what righteousness is **not.** The Pharisees had a system that was based on works and merit. If you performed the right sacrifices at the right time at the right place, following the strict regulations that had been developed over time, you were considered righteous. It was all focused on the external, paying little

---

14   Ray Pritchard, in his sermon "Full Stomachs and Empty Hearts", January 1996, http://www.keepbelieving.com/sermon/1996-01-28-Full-Stomachs-and-Empty-Hearts/.

or no attention to the inner workings of the heart. But the prophet Jeremiah reminds us, "The heart is deceitful above all things and beyond cure. Who can understand it?" (Jer. 17:9). So Jesus steps up and raises the bar by saying, "you need to exceed the righteousness of the Pharisees." His listeners probably thought to themselves, "How is that possible?"

Again we find help waiting only a few verses later at the beginning of Matthew 6: "Be careful not to practice your righteousness in front of others to be seen by them. If you do, you will have no reward from your Father in heaven" (Matt. 6:1). This must have caused the religious leaders listening to cringe. These powerful men loved to parade their works in public for all to see. They made a great show of their acts of charity, reveling in the praise of man. But Jesus points His followers in a very different direction. True righteousness doesn't seek the praise of man, but instead desires the favor of God.

Our final verse is also found in Matthew 6. "But seek first his kingdom and his righteousness, and all these things will be given to you as well" (Matt. 6:33). Like a laser beam, Jesus shifts the focus from external acts to the motives of the heart. What are your main priorities? What passions shape your dreams? Thinking back to the beginning of this chapter, what are the strongest appetites that fuel your actions? Maybe it's the drive to reach the top of the ladder in your profession. Perhaps it's a desire to meet the right person and fall in love. Or possibly it's a passion to accumulate great wealth before you die. Although these may be strong motivators, Jesus says they are not the most important. If it's not God's Kingdom and His righteousness you're seeking, then you are chasing after the wrong things. When we look at Matthew 5:6 in its entire context, we begin to understand that "seeking righteousness" involves making God's Word the standard by which you live your life. It means your deepest spiritual hunger and greatest spiritual thirst is to please the God who created you for His purposes.

Ray Pritchard says it this way, "Put these four passages together and what do you have? We are to hunger and thirst after 1) a truly Christian lifestyle, 2) that changes us from the inside out, 3) so that we no longer seek the praise of men, 4) but causes us to seek God's approval above everything else. This kind of life is possible for all of us. In fact, Jesus plainly says that anyone who lives this way is blessed by God."[15]

DRIVEN BY HUNGER

My wife, Sonia, grew up in the countries of El Salvador and Guatemala. As a young girl, she often went to bed at night with no dinner. She remembers times when she had to put a piece of wood between her teeth to bite on, because the pain in her stomach was so great. As Americans, we hear stories like this and shake our heads. We live in a country where (relatively speaking) very few people really know what it is like to experience true hunger. As I write these words, I am ashamed to admit how many times in my life I have said "I'm starving," when in reality it had only been a few hours since I had eaten my last snack or meal. Because of our lack of experience in this area, I'm afraid we often miss the urgency of Jesus' words in this text. We don't really know what it's like to truly hunger or thirst after something. But a quote from Proverbs reminds us of an

---

15   Ibid.

important principle we talked about earlier in this chapter: "The appetite of laborers works for them, their hunger drives them on" (Prov. 16:26). Hunger is a powerful motivator of human behavior. When our appetite is for the things of God's Kingdom, we have immense power working to transform our hearts and minds. And according to Jesus, one of the fruits of this type of transformation is the righteousness of God in our lives.

But herein lies our real problem. We are so busy filling ourselves up on the junk food of this world that we don't have any room left to eat the delicacies offered to us as part of God's Kingdom. We are spiritually malnourished, and we don't even know it. When I lived in Guatemala as a missionary, I had an experience that helps illustrate our condition. I had gone several weeks feeling tired and exhausted. Every time I was thirsty, I would reach for coffee or soda pop to quench my thirst and hopefully increase my energy. The problem was that my body, in order to function properly, wanted and needed *water*. So every time I drank more coffee, instead of quenching my body's thirst, I was dehydrating myself even further—it got so serious that I actually passed out. And a doctor later informed me that my heart had almost stopped completely! I had so seriously misunderstood and misdirected my thirst that I had caused myself to become seriously sick.

The same thing happens to us spiritually when we misdirect our hunger and thirst for God. We spend great amounts of time and energy pursuing the temporary things of this world (money, sex, power, entertainment, status, etc.) only to find ourselves empty and unsatisfied. As a result, we have no energy left to pursue the eternal truths that God promises will satisfy every longing of our hearts.

Thankfully, Jesus doesn't leave us here with no hope of escaping the power of our misplaced appetites. Instead, He points us toward the promises of God's provision.

THE FULLNESS OF GOD'S PROVISION

This Beatitude ends with a life-giving promise: "they will be filled." This is not a minor truth to be skipped over; this is a life-transforming promise to be embraced. Our Lord tells us, just as plainly as He can, that when we begin to hunger and thirst after Him and His Kingdom, he will personally make sure we get filled. But the logical question then follows: "Filled with what?" Is Jesus talking about food, or water, or money, or power, or personal happiness? No. He is talking about righteousness; you and I will be filled with righteousness. As Ray Pritchard explains,

> Let me go out on a limb and make a bold statement. Whatever you want in the spiritual realm, you can have if you want it badly enough. I don't think we appreciate the importance of this truth. Most of us are about as close to God right now as we want to be. We have about as much joy as we want. We have about as much peace as we want. For the most part, you are where you are right now because that's where you want to be. If you were hungry for something better from God, you could have it.
>
> - If you want it, you can have a close walk with God.
>
> - If you want it, you can have a better marriage.
>
> - If you want to, you can do God's will.
>
> - If you want to, you can grow spiritually.

- If you want to, you can become a man or a woman of God.

- If you want to, you can change deeply ingrained habits.

- If you want to, you can break destructive patterns of behavior.[16]

I want you to take a minute and think about a Christian whom you really admire. Maybe it's one of the great heroes of the faith you've read about, someone like Dwight Moody, Amy Carmichael, or Charles Spurgeon. Maybe it's someone you've spent time with who has really challenged you to trust God. Whoever it is you look up to in the faith, what makes this person different than you? The answer is nothing, other than the level of his or her hunger for God!

BILL BRIGHT

Let me give you an illustration of what this looks like in real life. Bill Bright, who lived from 1921 to 2003, was just an ordinary man who happened to develop an extraordinary hunger for God. In 1956 he started a ministry called Campus Crusade for Christ. Over the next 50 years, his ministry grew to be the largest Christian ministry in the world. Bright credits its incredible growth to his overwhelming passion to present the love and claims of Jesus Christ to "every living person on earth." God honored his hunger and passion. As the world's largest Christian ministry, Campus Crusade for Christ serves people in 191 countries through a staff of 26,000 full-time employees and more than 225,000 trained volunteers working in some 60 niche ministries and projects, ranging from military

---

16   Ibid.

ministry to inner city ministry.[17] There is nothing extraordinary about Bill Bright, other than his passion and hunger for God.

What a perfect example of what we just learned above. "We have as much of the things of God as we want." What is keeping you or me from experiencing this same level of God's power in our lives? According to Jesus' words in our text, the only thing keeping us from being filled up spiritually like Dr. Bright is the level of our own hunger and thirst for righteousness.

A FINAL THOUGHT

This is not the only place our Lord uses the images of hunger and thirst in the Gospels. For example, "Then Jesus declared, 'I am the bread of life. Whoever comes to me will never go *hungry,* and whoever believes in me will never be *thirsty*'" (John 6:35; italics mine). One of the most basic and beautiful truths of the Christian faith is the intimate relationship that Jesus offers to His followers. By tying these two texts together, we become aware that the call for us to hunger and thirst after righteousness is actually a call for us to desire a closer and more personal relationship with Jesus Christ.

Do you realize what this means? When Jesus says we will be filled, He is literally talking about filling our lives with more of His presence. Listen to how Paul describes this truth in Romans. "But if Christ is in you, then even though your body is subject to death because of sin, the Spirit gives life because of righteousness" (Rom. 8:10). By adding a couple of pronouns in parentheses to the text, we can get an even clearer picture of Paul's emphasis. When our lives are filled with the presence and power of our Lord, the

---

17   "William R. "Bill" Bright, Founder of World's Largest Christian Ministry Dies," Campus Crusade for Christ, July 19, 2003, http://billbright.ccci.org/public/.

"Spirit gives (us) life because of (His) righteousness." This is where the new life promised to believers finds its power. When we hunger and thirst for righteousness, Jesus Himself becomes the source of our righteousness, filling us up on the inside through the presence of the Holy Spirit. Even though our bodies will one day experience physical death, because of the presence of the Spirit of God, we now have the promise of eternal life.

GOING DEEPER

1) Can you honestly say, "I am experiencing a growing hunger for the things of God's Kingdom?"

2) Do you sense God's Spirit changing your heart, or is your focus more on external issues?

3) Can you honestly say, "I am more interested in pleasing God than I am in pleasing men?"

If you can answer these questions in the affirmative, you are growing in righteousness. And according to the promise of Jesus in Matthew 5:6, you will be filled with the power and presence of Jesus Christ!

CHAPTER 6

THE POWER
OF MERCY

Blessed are the merciful, for they will be shown mercy.

Matthew 5:7

AN OUTWARD FOCUS

IT'S HERE, IN THE FIFTH Beatitude, that we begin to realize an important truth; not only do these powerful teachings affect our relationship with a holy God, but when taken to heart, they should also transform the way we interact with the people in our everyday lives. Understanding this shift in focus is essential to understanding Jesus' message in this text. The first four Beatitudes force us to admit our broken condition and complete dependence on God's amazing mercy and grace. When we are poor in spirit, we admit our need for Him. When we mourn, we see the cost of our sin through the sacrifice Jesus made for us on the cross. This leads us to meekness—a willingness to give up the illusion of self-sufficiency, instead gladly surrendering control of our lives to our Lord, Jesus Christ. Once we have moved through these first three steps, the

result is a deep hunger and thirst for a personal relationship with
God that Jesus calls *righteousness* (defined in the last chapter as "a
truly Christian lifestyle that changes us from the inside out, so that
we no longer seek the praise of men, but instead seek God's approval
above everything else").[18] Now that we have a clear understanding
of what it takes to be restored into a right relationship with God,
Jesus shifts the focus in the next four Beatitudes outward. How does
this new relationship with God affect our relationships with the
people around us?

DEFINING MERCY

Jesus begins to answer this question in verse 7, "Blessed are the
merciful, for they will be shown mercy" (Matt. 5:7). Probably
the biggest stumbling block most Christians face when trying to
live out this verse is a complete misunderstanding of what the
word *mercy* actually means. We have a tendency to dumb down
and slowly change the way we use words in our culture. For example, the word *awesome* is supposed to be reserved for someone
or something (usually God) that actually inspires awe. But sadly,
in today's vernacular, you are just as likely to hear the word
awesome used to describe a piece of apple pie as to describe the
works of God. And we find the same difficulty in the ways we
misuse the word *mercy*. The 1828 version of Webster's dictionary
defined *mercy* as:

1. That benevolence, mildness or tenderness of heart
    which disposes a person to overlook injuries, or to treat

---

18   Pritchard, "Full Stomachs" (sermon).

an offender better than he deserves . . . Mercy is a distinguishing attribute of the Supreme Being.

The Lord is long-suffering and of great mercy, forgiving iniquity and transgression, and by no means clearing the guilty. Num. 14.

2. An act or exercise of mercy or favor. It is a mercy that they escaped.

   I am not worthy of the least of all thy mercies. Gen. 32.

3. Pity; compassion manifested towards a person in distress.

   And he said, he that showed mercy on him. Luke. 10.

4. Clemency and bounty.

   Mercy and truth preserve the king; and his throne is upheld by mercy. Prov. 28.

5. Charity, or the duties of charity and benevolence.

   I will have mercy and not sacrifice. Matt. 9.

6. Grace; favor. 1 Cor. 7. Jude 2.

7. Eternal life, the fruit of mercy. 2 Tim. 1.

8. Pardon.

   I cry thee mercy with all my heart.

9. The act of sparing, or the forbearance of a violent act expected. The prisoner cried for mercy.[19]

Throughout this definition, the Bible is used as the primary source of reference. Every line has a Scripture quotation cited. Mercy was clearly understood in light of a holy God who could

---

19 Webster's 1828 American Dictionary Online, s.v. "mercy," accessed July 2013, http://1828.mshaffer.com/d/search/word,mercy.

not look upon sin. According to these biblical definitions, mercy is primarily reserved for someone who is guilty of something.

However, today's online dictionaries have a slightly—but significantly— different definition:

1. compassionate or kindly forbearance shown toward an offender, an enemy, or other person in one's power; compassion, pity, or benevolence: Have mercy on the poor sinner.

2. the disposition to be compassionate or forbearing: an adversary wholly without mercy.

3. the discretionary power of a judge to pardon someone or to mitigate punishment, especially to send to prison rather than invoke the death penalty.

4. an act of kindness, compassion, or favor: She has performed countless small mercies for her friends and neighbors.

5. something that gives evidence of divine favor; blessing: It was just a mercy we had our seat belts on when it happened.[20]

Today's definition has a completely different feel than Noah Webster's 1828 version. Although it does use the phrase "have mercy on the poor sinner" in the first definition and the word "divine" in the last one, the overarching theme of a holy God, along with the emphasis on using Scripture to help define the world we live in, is missing. This modern definition could lead a person to think of *mercy* as merely feeling sorry for someone who is suffering

20   Dictionary.com, s.v. "mercy," accessed July 2013, http://dictionary.reference.com/browse/mercy.

unjustly. Now being sympathetic is certainly a good quality, but it does not express the proper depth of Jesus' meaning here. In the second chapter of James we read the following: "Suppose a brother or a sister is without clothes and daily food. If one of you says to them, 'Go in peace; keep warm and well fed,' but does nothing about their physical needs, what good is it?" (James 2:15–16). James asks a very important question here. "What good is it if you see someone in need and feel sorry for them, but do nothing to actually help them out? What good is your sympathy?"

Another word that is often equated with *mercy* is the word *kindness*. Certainly, as believers we are instructed to treat others with kindness. It's even described as a "fruit of the Spirit" in Galatians 5:22. Nevertheless, this biblical word still doesn't get at the heart of what Jesus means when he uses the words *merciful* and *mercy* in our text. We get some important help from a sermon by pastor Timothy Smith:

> The word Jesus uses for mercy is "eleos," and it is full of great meaning. It is used to describe an attribute of God. God is said to be "rich in mercy" (Eph. 2:4). Titus 3:5 tells us that we are saved by His mercy. And Peter tells us that: "In His great mercy he has given us new birth into a living hope" (1 Pet. 1:3). "Eleos" in its root carries the meaning, "to wash over." In Greek culture, wherein Jesus lived, it was used in the context of "whitewashing" a wall or "wiping out" an impurity or "canceling" a debt. You see mercy goes beyond sympathy to empathy. It is "love in action." [emphasis mine] You not only wash out the deed

that was done against you but, and here is the real challenge, you find a way to help the other person.[21]

What a great illustration to help us understand the mobilizing
power of mercy. Mercy causes us to move from sympathy to empa-
thy. It is love in action. It's not hard to see how this should apply to
our lives. A heart that is truly filled with mercy will not be satisfied
with vague feelings of sympathy, but will instead be driven to take
action. The thought process will look something like this: I see the
need. My heart is moved with compassion. How can I help bring
Jesus' message of hope and healing into this painful situation?

I'm going to go out on a limb here and make a prediction. I bet
that if you're willing to look around your community, you could
find at least one person or situation where God's mercy, displayed
through your actions, could bring health, healing, and hope!

THE HEBREW WORD FOR "MERCY"

Jesus grew up studying the Hebrew Scriptures. They framed His
understanding of the world and were an essential part of His teachings. For this reason it's also important to look at the Hebrew word
for *mercy*, which is *racham*. The Holman Bible dictionary defines
racham this way:

> Racham is related to the Hebrew word for "womb" and
> expresses a mother's (Isaiah 49:15) or father's (Ps. 103:13)
> love and compassion, a feeling of pity and devotion to a
> helpless child. **It is a deep emotional feeling seek-
> ing a concrete expression of love** (Genesis 43 14;

21   Timothy Smith, in his sermon "The Mercy That Shows Mercy", July 2006, http://
www.sermoncentral.com/sermons/the-mercy-that-shows-mercy-timothy-smith-
sermon-on-forgiveness-for-others-93288.asp.

Deuteronomy 13:17; emphasis mine). This word always expresses the feeling of the superior or more powerful for the inferior or less powerful and thus never expresses human feeling for God.[22]

Focusing on the highlighted area of this quote, I believe that, in the context of a mother's or father's compassion, the concrete expression of love that is being sought is a desire to take action and do something about the situation. Mercy transforms us from spectators who sit in the bleachers cheering, to players on the field who work desperately to affect the outcome of the game. And this is why I believe Jesus placed this beatitude here, after the first four that dealt with restoring our relationship to God. Because of our fallen nature, mercy is simply not possible in our own strength. It is only possible when you and I have a transformed heart. It is only possible when God is working through us. Mercy is not a reaction, but an action—born out of a regenerated heart! When a Christian displays mercy, they are reflecting one of the attributes of God. Consider the following verses (the highlights are mine):

> David said to Gad, "I am in deep distress. Let me fall into the hands of the LORD, **for his mercy is very great**; but do not let me fall into human hands." – 1 Chron. 21:13

> But in **your great mercy** you did not put an end to them or abandon them, for **you are a gracious and merciful God.** – Neh. 9:31

---

22   Holman Bible Dictionary, s.v. "compassion," accessed July 2103, http://www.studylight.org/dic/hbd/view.cgi?number=T1369.

Because of the tender mercy of our God, by which the rising sun will come to us from heaven. – Luke 1:78

It does not, therefore, depend on human desire or effort, **but on God's mercy.** – Rom. 9:16

But because of his great love for us, **God, who is rich in mercy** . . . – Eph. 2:4

Let us then approach God's throne of grace with confidence, **so that we may receive mercy** and find grace to help us in our time of need. – Heb. 4:16

He saved us, not because of righteous things we had done, **but because of his mercy.** – Titus 3:5a

The Lord is full of compassion and **mercy.**
– James 5:11b

These verses make it clear that God is merciful. So when you or I display mercy, we are reflecting God's very character to the world. This is the reciprocal part of Jesus' message in Matthew 5:7. As we receive God's mercy, we reflect that same mercy to those whom God places in our lives. The more mercy we reflect, the more mercy we discover coming down from God. In *The Merchant of Venice,* Shakespeare describes mercy as a gentle rain from heaven. This is a very helpful illustration for us to understand. Mercy comes down from above. It always starts with God, and then moves to man. Listen to how the Reverend Ralph Sockman describes this process:

The gentle rain seems a weak thing. But watch it falling on a plot of hard, dry, trampled earth. After awhile there is a softening, and life begins to push up through the mellowed ground. So with the mind of man. When we let thoughts of divine mercy drop repeatedly on the gardens of our imaginations, our hearts are softened. (Ralph Sockman, *The Higher Happiness*, p. 111)

I love this word picture. It helps me to visualize God's mercy falling down like rain on my heart, washing away the hardness caused by selfishness and pride. Slowly but surely, God's merciful rain accomplishes its purpose, revealing the soft and compassionate new heart that God has given me through Christ. Then as I am moved by mercy to take action on behalf of God's Kingdom here on earth, the more aware I become of God's continuing mercy raining down in my life.

THE DIFFERENCE BETWEEN MERCY AND GRACE

In Christian circles, we often use the words *grace* and *mercy* as if they mean exactly the same thing. But that is not correct; they have two distinct meanings. An easy way to remember the difference is to think about them in this way: *Mercy* is "not receiving what you do deserve" (the wrath of God); *grace* is "receiving what you don't deserve" (the righteousness of Christ). Grace forgives, and mercy helps restore. I really believe this is why Jesus chose to focus on mercy as the transitional step in the Beatitudes. When mercy becomes real in the hearts of God's people, it becomes a driving force in mobilizing the church to live in a way that honors the very heart of God.

My daughter Ana recently returned from a trip to India and Thailand. While she was there, she visited the home that Mother

Theresa started as a place to care for the people left to die in the streets of Calcutta. She also spent many hours working with a ministry that helps restore women who have been kidnapped and sold into sexual slavery. Once you've been to a place like Calcutta, where the overwhelming stench of human waste and death is everywhere, where the sheer number of people trying to survive is staggering, where the unbridled wickedness of human indifference to the suffering of others can be seen everywhere—you quickly realize there is no way that anyone, in their own strength and abilities, would ever choose this area of the world to live and serve God. But guess what? There are many Christians who do exactly that. Powered by God's grace and filled with God's mercy and love, these transformed Christians are able to overcome their own selfish, self-centered tendencies, enabling them to move out into a lost and broken world.

THE STORY OF THE GOOD SAMARITAN

One of the great examples of mercy in the Bible comes from the story of the Good Samaritan in Luke chapter 10. Jesus spoke this parable in response to some questions concerning the nature of eternal life. After Jesus confirmed the two most important commands, "to love God and to love your neighbor" (Luke 10:27), the discussion focused on a single question: "Who is my neighbor?" Without missing a beat, Jesus began talking about a man who was traveling from Jerusalem to Jericho. Because of the difficulty of the terrain and the numerous hiding spots along the way, this was a favorite staging area for robbers and thieves. No one with any knowledge of this area ever traveled this road alone. And in the words of Paul Harvey, "You know the rest of the story." While the man was traveling on the road, he was viciously attacked by men who took all his possessions. They also wounded him severely, leaving him for dead. Shortly thereafter, a priest (possibly on his way either to or from serving in the temple) came along and saw the poor man lying by the road. But instead of stopping to help, he ignored him and crossed over to the other side. A little while later, a Levite came by and did the same thing.

It's easy, at this point, to assume that the priest and the Levite were evil men. But that is not necessarily the case. They were simply trying to follow the Old Testament Law. As Jews, they were not to be defiled by anything that was unclean. Their problem was the same problem we can have today if we're not careful. We can be so focused on trying to stay clean from the filth of this world that we refuse to reach out and touch people we view as unclean. It is easy to look at people who aren't part of the "Christian club" and conclude that they're getting what they deserve. But by trying to follow the strict letter of the Law, these two men were missing the very heart of God.

It's here where Jesus' story takes an ironic twist. Along comes this half-breed Samaritan, a man who any decent law-abiding Jew would despise, yet he is the one who stops and has mercy on the wounded man along the road. What an insult to the lawyer who had asked Jesus the questions that started this parable! And interestingly, this is why, at the end of the story when Jesus asks the question "Which man was a neighbor?", the lawyer answered, "The one who showed mercy on him"—instead of saying "the Samaritan." Even after hearing this powerful parable, he still couldn't bring himself to say the word "Samaritan." That is how much hatred and animosity existed between these two groups of people.

But in Jesus' story it was the Samaritan who stopped. It was the Samaritan who saw the man, bound up his wounds, put the man on his donkey, took him to an inn, and took care of him. Before he left, he also gave the innkeeper two silver coins and told him to look after the man until he returned. And in one final insult to His audience, Jesus concludes His story with a promise by the Samaritan to return and pay for any extra expenses that the innkeeper might incur. Think about what this man was willing to do, and all for a man he had never met: a man who, if the tables were turned, probably would not have done the same for him. What a perfect picture of the power of mercy.

This parable powerfully challenges us about application. How can we begin to reflect the kind of mercy that Jesus talks about in this story? The kind of mercy that Jesus says (in Matthew 5:7) will lead to God's mercy being poured back into our lives. I think the application starts when we realize that according to Jesus, all three of these men "happened" upon the man by the side of the road. In other words, no one went out looking for a wounded stranger to help. It simply happened. And as a result, we see the revelation of God's mercy, which was already dwelling in the transformed heart of the Samaritan.

Hopefully the application is clear: this is the way it will happen in our lives as well. We will be going about our own business, and an opportunity to help someone in need will arise. Not necessarily someone we know. Not necessarily someone who can pay us back later. Not necessarily someone we feel great affection for. But someone who is nevertheless in desperate need of our help. It's at this point that the condition of our hearts will be revealed. What will I do? How will I show mercy? The priest had a chance, the Levite had a chance, the Samaritan had a chance; they all "happened" upon the helpless man. But only one man—the man judged least likely by the world's standards—is the man who stopped to help.

As this parable ends, Jesus says something extremely important to the lawyer: "Go and do likewise." In case there is still any question about our marching orders, Jesus drives home His point. As His followers, we are to "go and do likewise." As we receive mercy, we are to be conduits of that mercy to the people we encounter every day. Life is full of opportunities for us to demonstrate mercy. All it takes is a believer who is willing to look.

Ray Pritchard sums it up well when he says, "Jesus died to create a race of merciful men and women—people who have received mercy and now gladly give it away to others. You and I are called to be those people!"[23] This is an incredible challenge to me as a Christian, and I pray it is to you as well. If I were to go to your home, to your work place, to the people who know you best, and ask them if they see the mercy of God reflected in your life, how do you think they would answer? What if I were to go out into your community and ask the same question about how your neighbors see your church? What do you think they would say? I don't know about you, but I believe I still have a long way to go in this area. I believe that we as the church need to do some real soul searching.

23   Ray Pritchard, in his sermon "What We Saw in India", February 1996, http://www. keepbelieving.com/sermon/1996-02-18-What-We-Saw-In-India/.

It's time that Jesus' words in Matthew 5:7 become more than a nice sounding verse to post on Facebook. It's time these words became the hallmark of what the church represents to the lost and broken world in which we live.

CONCLUSION

The first four Beatitudes focused on how we can begin to experience the cure for what ails our broken hearts: through a personal relationship with Jesus Christ. But starting with Matthew 5:7, Jesus shifts the focus outward: "If you want to be my disciples, then start living like it!" His message in the Beatitudes is just too powerful for us to keep to ourselves. By its very nature, it compels us to take action. And so it's here at this juncture where we realize an important truth: the cure is bigger than our individual lives. It's time for us to go out and share this new life we have received. One of the primary ways we're called to do this is by reflecting the mercy we've received to those—like ourselves—who deserve it the least. *"Blessed are the merciful, for they will be shown mercy."*

GOING DEEPER

★Take a few minutes to read the story of the Good Samaritan in Luke 10.

1) Why do you think this story is so powerful to read?

2) How might imitating the kind of mercy displayed by the Samaritan in this story help to heal some of the broken relationships in your life?

3) Why is it so hard to show mercy to people who we think are paying the consequences for decisions they have made?

4) Think back to the last time you saw someone in desperate need: for example, a driver stranded along the road alone at night, or a homeless person with a sign asking for food. How did you respond? How different might your life be if God responded to you the same way?

5) Why is the characteristic of mercy so important in living the life Jesus emphasizes in the Beatitudes?

CHAPTER 7

I CAN SEE CLEARLY NOW!

Blessed are the pure in heart, for they will see God.

Matthew 5:8

LEARNING TO SEE GOD

HAVE YOU EVER TAKEN THE time to think about the incredible nature of our Lord's promise here in the sixth Beatitude? If you develop a pure heart, you will see God! I don't know about you, but when I begin to chew on that thought, I get really excited! Jesus is offering you and me an opportunity to see God! This is such a staggering promise that I want to make sure we clearly understand what our Lord is saying. Is it really possible to see God?

My first thoughts when I hear this promise take me to Psalm 19:1, "The heavens declare the glory of God; the skies proclaim the work of his hands." I don't understand how anyone can look around at this world we live in and believe that it all "somehow" happened by chance. The fall colors this year were spectacular.

Why do we even have colors? Why is the human eye even able to detect the differences between red, yellow, orange, and green? Why do these colors affect our thoughts and emotions so deeply?

I am convinced that the reason why is simple. Just like the psalm says, God reveals Himself to us through His creation. One of the most basic ways we get to see God is through the beauty and integrity of the things He's made. But sadly, when our hearts are hard and we are full of ourselves, we don't take the time to see Him. Before I became a Christian, I believed evolution was responsible for the world as we see it today. Somehow I didn't see God, even when I looked around at creation. But now, after my conversion and the transformation that He has wrought in my heart and mind, I see God everywhere. It's like the lyrics to that old Johnny Nash song from the early seventies,

> I can see clearly now, the rain is gone,
> I can see all obstacles in my way
> Gone are the dark clouds that had me blind
> It's gonna be a bright (bright), bright (bright)
> Sun-Shiny day.[24]

I bet you can hear the tune in your head as you read those words. The first time I heard that song after I got saved, I felt like he was describing what I was feeling. The world that seemed so hopeless before, now seemed full of potential. The things of God that used to seem so distant and foggy were now crystal clear! Once we enter

---

24   Johnny Nash, "I Can See Clearly Now," 1972, Epic Records.

into a personal relationship with Jesus Christ, the Holy Spirit begins to open our eyes to God's activity in and around our lives.

Do you understand the significance of this truth? To see God is not necessarily talking about when we get to heaven. As Christians, that day will certainly come. But in this text, I believe Jesus is also talking about seeing God in the here and now. As David Yarbrough points out, "The pure in heart will begin to see God in everything. Not just in nature, but also in their circumstances, both good and bad, in their families, their churches, their schools, their jobs, and the list could go on forever."[25]

DEFINING THE WORD PURE

So what does Jesus mean when He talks about a pure heart? Let's start with the word *pure*. Look at the label on a bar of Ivory soap. What does it say in big letters in the bottom left corner? *PURE*. Why would a company put the word *PURE* on the front of their soap package? Evidently, they believe there's something about that word that will cause us to buy their product.

So what exactly is it that makes something pure? Have you ever reached into the fridge, grabbed hold of a carton of milk, taken a big gulp and realized that the milk was starting to turn sour? What was your reaction? You couldn't get the milk out of your mouth fast enough! Now why is that? The answer is easy—because the milk is no longer pure. It's contaminated, and your mouth makes sure your brain is aware of the situation. Let me ask you another question. Have you ever been driving down the highway and gotten stuck

---

25   David Yarbrough, in his sermon "The Way To Purity", February 2002, http://www. sermoncentral.com/sermons/the-way-to-purity-david-yarbrough-sermon-on-sermon-on-the-mount-43176.asp.

behind a large diesel truck that's spewing black smoke? What is your immediate reaction? You look in your mirrors to make sure the passing lanes are clear, and then you step on the gas and go! Why? As long as you're stuck behind that truck, the air in your car is not pure. As we see in these examples, in most areas of our lives, purity is very important to us. And it certainly was in Jesus' day as well.

Similar to these illustrations, when Jesus uses the word *pure*, it carries the idea of something that is clean, free from contamination, and unmixed. So when Jesus tells us in Matthew 5:8, "blessed are the pure in heart, for they will see God," He is challenging us to take a look at the condition of our hearts. Is my heart clean? Is it undefiled by the filth of this world? Do I guard my heart from contamination? In *The Message*, which is a modern paraphrase of the Bible, Eugene Peterson translates it this way, "You're blessed when you get your inside world—your mind and heart—put right. Then you can see God in the outside world."

I hope you are beginning to grasp how life-changing this truth can be. I remember reading Henry Blackaby's wonderful book *Experiencing God* in 1998, about one year after I became a Christian. This book greatly affected my life. As I read the study and answered the questions, my eyes were opened to just how personal our relationship with God can be. Blackaby's central thesis in this book hits on this very point. When we stop focusing on ourselves, and begin focusing on what God has revealed to us about Himself, we can't help but start to see His activity in the world around us. God is actively working in this world, seeking to draw the lost.

As Christians, we are given the opportunity to join God in His work. As we see His activity, we experience a moment Blackaby calls "a crisis of faith." Will we be "obedient and join God in His work," or will we let fear and unbelief rob us of the opportunity of "Experiencing God."[26] What I discovered was amazing. The more I would respond in faith, the more I would experience God's power. The more I would experience God's power, the more my heart was conformed to His image. I began to realize that, slowly but surely, His desires were becoming the desires of my heart. Now I'm certainly not saying that I have arrived and I always do God's will, but this study helped me begin a journey that continues to this day. A journey that has allowed me to "see God" in ways I never imagined were possible.

Notice that the emphasis here is on what's inside us—in the heart. In Jesus' day, people thought of the heart as the very center of a person. Your thoughts, feelings, motivations, and passions all flowed out of your heart. The heart was seen as the center of who a person really was. If you wanted to know what was going on inside of someone, you only had to look at what kinds of actions flowed out of his or her heart. And this is where we find our most basic problem. The Bible warns us that "the heart is deceitful above all things and beyond cure. Who can understand it?" (Jer. 17:9). In our fallen state, we cannot trust our hearts to lead us toward God. Indeed, according to this text, just the opposite is true. We deny God and try to take His place. Our problem is not hard to grasp: we don't even know our own hearts. Only the power of God can reveal

26   Henry Blackaby and Claude King, *Experiencing God* (Nashville, TN: B&H Publishing, 2008), 207-209.

the true condition of a heart. Like carpenter ants in the foundation of a house, sin can get into our hearts and slowly eat away at the base of our spiritual life. But this is where things get tricky. Just like with the house, what's going on inside us may not immediately be apparent on the outside. To the rest of the world it may appear that our outside life is healthy, when in reality our inner spiritual life is rotting at its foundation.

OUR NEW HEART

This is why the new heart we are given at the time of salvation is central to our ability to see God. Without our new heart's inherent purity (a purity we don't possess in our own right, but a purity we are given as part of our new relationship to Jesus Christ) we can never see or understand the things of God. But once we begin to walk in the newness of life, guided by the presence of the Holy Spirit in our hearts, our eyes are opened so we can see God's works more clearly. This process is explained in detail in Ezekiel 34: "Then I will sprinkle clean water on you, and you shall be clean; I will cleanse you from all your filthiness and from all your idols. I will give you a new heart and put a new spirit within you; I will take the heart of stone out of your flesh and give you a heart of flesh. I will put My Spirit within you and cause you to walk in My statutes, and you will keep My judgments and do them" (Ezek. 34:25–27 NKJV). When a person receives Jesus Christ as Lord, they not only receive a new life, but also a new heart. This new heart is different from their old heart. It's not hardened by sin like their old heart of stone. This new heart is soft and receptive to the Holy Spirit. And most importantly, this new heart has both the desire to see God and the ability to follow His ways. (For a deeply satisfying study of this topic, I recommend the book *Revolution Within* by Dwight Edwards).[27]

This truth sets the stage for another truth that is hard for us to grasp. When God looks at you and me, He is not concerned about our outward appearance. That always comes as a great shock to people who spend much of their time and energy focusing on that area. I'm not saying that God has no concern for your outside (taking good care of our bodies is part of good stewardship), but His primary focus is on your inside. And now the reason is clear. What's in your heart will be reflected in every other area of your life. "For as he thinketh in his heart, so is he" (Prov. 23:7a KJV). It all boils down to what's happening on the inside.

JESUS AND THE PHARISEES

There is no doubt that Jesus understood our propensity to focus on the outside, ignoring the work that the Holy Spirit wants to do on the inside. We see this in the way He responded to some of the people of his day, people whose main focus was on how they appeared to others. The Pharisees knew exactly what to wear out in public, what to pray when others were listening, and how much to give when the crowds were watching. They loved to make a show of their outward purity. But in Matthew 15, we see Jesus' response:

> You hypocrites! Isaiah was right when he prophesied about you: "These people honor me with their lips, but their hearts are far from Me. They worship me in vain; their teachings are merely human rules." Jesus called the crowd to him and said, "Listen and understand. What

---

27   Dwight Edwards, *Revolution Within: A Fresh Look at Supernatural Living* (Colorado Springs, CO: Waterbrook, 2002).

goes into someone's mouth does not defile them, but what comes out of their mouth, that is what defiles them."
– Matt. 15:7–11

Jesus saw past all the fluff, and looked directly into their hearts. His response says it all: it's not your lips but your heart that I want.

This was not Jesus' only confrontation with this group. He took another opportunity to point out their hypocrisy when He called them "white-washed tombs." This must have outraged the Pharisees. These were people who took great pride in their outward cleanliness, but Jesus compared their insides to "rotting corpses." While carefully following the letter of the Law on the outside, they had allowed their insides to rot. Their hearts were infested with anger, envy, unforgiveness, bitterness, and most of all, pride. Still driving the point home, Jesus says, "For out of the heart come evil thoughts, murder, adultery, sexual immorality, theft, false testimony, slander. These are what defile a person; but eating with unwashed hands does not defile them" (Matt. 15:19–20). Jesus was fed up with their hypocrisy. They may have been able to fool themselves, but they were not going to pull one over on God!

With these verses as a backdrop, we begin to get a clearer understanding of what Jesus means by having a pure heart. He's not simply referring to a "right" belief system (although that's important), and He's not referring to taking the "right" actions (although those are also important). He's talking about having the right belief system and taking the right actions with the right motivations as the fuel in our hearts! The key is the motivation. Are you fueled by pride and selfishness, or are you fueled by a passion for God's glory?

LIVING IT OUT

Let me give you some practical examples of what this might look like in your everyday life. If you come to church on Sunday morning—participating in the praise, joining in with the worship, dutifully taking notes during the teaching, and hugging everyone during the time of fellowship—but then act like everyone else at work on Monday morning—gossiping, telling dirty jokes, ignoring people who require extra effort to love—then Jesus says you're a hypocrite, and your worship is in vain. If you put on your best spiritual face in front of your church body, but act dishonestly by stealing (even little things like office supplies) from your employer when no one is looking, then Jesus says you're a hypocrite, and your spiritual acts are in vain. If you teach your children about sexual purity, but look at pornography online when you're home alone, then Jesus says you're a hypocrite, and your pretension of purity is in vain. If you tell everyone you love God, but you celebrate the misfortune of an annoying neighbor whose actions drive you crazy, then Jesus says you're a hypocrite, and your love is in vain. This is why purity of heart is more than just a "right" belief system and taking the "right" actions. It's the integrity of heart that causes your actions to line up with what you believe.

Now you may be wondering, how is this possible? I want to be pure, but I don't seem to be able to stop from doing the things I know are wrong, the things that contaminate my heart. This is why Jesus' words in Matthew 5 are so important. This is not something we can do on our own. We are all terminally ill. We all have a condition that is robbing us of spiritual life, making our hearts unclean before a Holy God. The first step toward finding the cure is to accept that we have this sinful condition and acknowledge that we need God's help to be made clean, and to become pure. And here is where the beauty of Jesus' words can help set us free. Purity isn't only the absence of corruption in your heart. It's also the blessing of God's power and presence in your everyday life. If we could cleanse ourselves in our own strength, then we wouldn't turn to God. We would instead trust in our own good works. We would end up acting self-righteously, just as the Pharisees did in Jesus' day.

The path to purity of heart must pass through the first five Beatitudes: a poor spirit that admits its need for God, a willingness to mourn our sin, the meekness to surrender our life to God's control, the hunger and thirst for a right relationship with God (righteousness), and a heart softened by the gentle and consistent rain of God's mercy. It starts with a brutally honest assessment of who we are apart from the transforming work of Jesus Christ.

At this point, you may be wondering if this journey is worth it? Jesus' answer in Matthew 5:7 is quite clear: *"Blessed are the pure in heart, for they will see God."* The journey is worth it—if you want to see God! And so here we are, back at our Lord's incredible promise: the pure in heart will see God.

When we surrender our hearts to God's Spirit, His presence begins to manifest itself in our lives. And now, instead of a divided heart which is constantly torn between two masters, more and more of our heart begins to respond to God. Our deepest desires are no longer for the grubby things of this world, things that rob us of life. Because God has changed our hearts, we actually desire to do God's will. As we do God's will, we can't help but see God's hand all around us in the world. Are you beginning to grasp the depth of God's promise to you? You and I don't have to live shallow, self-centered, and self-focused lives. We don't have to go through the motions. We don't need to wallow in the mud! God has created each of us for so much more than we are currently experiencing!

CONCLUSION

In order to close this chapter properly, we need to peek ahead a couple of chapters to Jesus' own description of the transformation that takes place through the principles we've been studying in the Beatitudes. He tells us that we will become "salt and light" for a corrupt and dark world. Salt stops corruption, and light overcomes the darkness. In essence, Jesus is promising us that when our hearts become pure, the very character and nature of God will be reflected in our everyday lives. Not only will our purity of heart help us to see God, but others will begin to see God in us as well!

Being pure in heart doesn't come from hiding away in a monastery. It doesn't come from keeping ourselves hidden from the pain and suffering of the world. If that were the case, Jesus never would have spent His time helping the poor, the needy, the sick, or the outcasts. He would have been worried that they would make Him unclean. But because He understood that His purity comes from a right relationship with the Father and is fueled by a transformed heart, He knew that the filth of this world had no chance against a deep passion for God's will to be done!

GOING DEEPER

I want to finish this chapter where I started it, with Matthew 5:7: *"Blessed are the pure in heart, for they will see God."* When your heart truly becomes pure on the inside, you can't help but see God everywhere on the outside.

Here are some questions to help you apply this important truth to your life.

1) What about your family? Which family members need to see God's love working through your pure heart?

2) How different might your relationship be with your spouse, your children, your brothers and sisters, if your heart was truly washed clean from anger, from unforgiveness, from coarse humor, and from selfish motives?

3) How different might your work or school environment be if you could reflect the heart of God, instead of reflecting the selfishness and pride of our culture?

4) What if your entire church body began seeking this purity of heart together? What might happen in your community? Is it possible that you would see God's transforming power start changing lives by redeeming the lost, restoring broken families, healing the sick, delivering those caught up in addiction, and comforting those overcome by depression and guilt?

5) Is it possible that, if you began seeking God with a real desire for change, His purity would wash you clean on the inside, so you could reflect Him on the outside to the people God places in your path?

CHAPTER 8

FIGHTING FOR PEACE

Blessed are the peacemakers, for they will be called sons of God.

Matthew 5:9

IS PEACE POSSIBLE?

WHEN WE TAKE A CLOSE look at the world in which we live, this is a tough text to make sense of. It almost seems as if the opposite is true. I think you could make a very strong case that in today's world it's dangerous to be a peacemaker. In the past few months of 2013 alone, there have been at least eight people killed and four-teen people wounded, simply because they were attempting to help bring peace to areas devastated by war (four Americans were killed in the US consulate in Libya, four UN peacekeepers were killed and eight wounded in Sudan, six UN peacekeepers were wounded in the Democratic Republic of the Congo), and in each case, the attacks that killed or wounded these individuals were unprovoked.

Unfortunately, this is nothing new. At the end of WWII, the most powerful nations of the world got together and decided it was time to end human conflict. As a symbol of this new era of peace, they commissioned a monument to be built in New York City. This monument contains a slightly modified verse from the Bible, referencing a future world peace. The statue boldly proclaims: "We shall beat our swords into plowshares." The implications of this statement are clear: mankind, through the coordinated efforts of the UN, will bring about conditions that will ensure world peace. No longer will men need to make our own weapons of war. The ones that already exist can be turned into farm tools. Our technological advances can be used to help our neighbors instead of to kill them. What a great and lofty ideal!

But the problem, of course, is that God is left out of this equation. When attempting to use the quote from Isaiah, they forgot the most important part of the verse. In its entirety, Isaiah 2:4 says, "He will judge between the nations and will settle disputes for many peoples. They will beat their swords into plowshares and their spears into pruning hooks. Nation will not take up sword against nation, nor will they train for war anymore." Nowhere in this verse do we see any indication that mankind will ever bring about peace on his own. This will be the ultimate work of God, through our Lord Jesus Christ.

Shortly after its inception in 1945, the UN began concentrating its efforts to create worldwide peace on the countries that make up the Middle East. This area includes Israel, Jordan, Iran, Iraq, Egypt, Syria, Lebanon, Libya, and the Palestinian people. What exactly has been the result of all this effort to create peace? In these 67 years of "peacemaking," there have been no less than 52 separate wars or uprisings, and thousands of terrorist attacks.[28] So what is the root cause of all these wars that threaten each generation of human beings? Many people have tried to answer this question, but most have been unsuccessful. However, when we turn to the Scriptures, we find that the answer has been sitting right in front of our eyes. James, the brother of Jesus, cuts right to the chase, "Where do wars and fights come from among you? Do they not come from your desires for pleasure that war in your members? You lust and do not have. You murder and covet and cannot obtain. You fight and war" (James 4:1–2a NKJV).

Man's history of war has to do with his human nature. We have a terminal disease that is spiritual in nature. Until we are able to admit our condition, we will not find the cure. Time after time, in century after century, nations have become more powerful than their neighbors, eventually coveting their territory and wealth. The sinful human heart always wants what others have, and sadly, it is willing to go to war to get it! So as a result, our world always seems to be on the edge of war. Iran and North Korea are both on the verge of obtaining the technology to create atomic bombs. Economic unrest, which used to be contained to third world countries, is now sweeping through the capital cities of Europe. The question is no longer, "Will there be war?", but instead, "When will the next war start?"

In 1984, the Gallup Organization was commissioned by CBN to ask Americans "What one question people would ask God if given the opportunity?" Not surprisingly, the number one response

---

28   TeachMideast: An Educational Initiative of the Middle East Policy Council, Time line of the Middle East in the 20th Century, http://www.teachmideast.org/essays/28-history/42-timeline-of-the-middle-east-in-the-20th-century.

was, "Will there ever be lasting world peace?" When you consider that an estimated two hundred million people (that is 200,000,000, just in case the number did not register) were killed by war in the twentieth century alone,[29] you realize this is an important question. Even with all of our advances in the area of technology, mankind doesn't seem to be able to get any closer to this elusive idea of world peace. In fact, just the opposite is true. With every positive advance comes the realization that what can be used for good can equally be used for evil. Instead of saving the world, technology has led to new and more devastating ways to kill each other.

WHAT THE BIBLE SAYS ABOUT PEACE

So what does the Bible have to say about the possibility of world peace? The answer may surprise you. The Bible has a lot to say about peace. The word itself appears over four hundred times. Jesus (prophesied as the Messiah) is referred to as "the Prince of Peace" (Isaiah 9:6). On the night He was born, the angels declared, "peace on earth" (Luke 2:14 KJV). When Jesus was preparing to leave His disciples He promised, "Peace I leave with you; my peace I give you. I do not give to you as the world gives. Do not let your hearts be troubled and do not be afraid" (John 14:27). And finally, Paul makes this amazing claim: "For he himself [Jesus] is our peace, who has made the two groups one and has destroyed the barrier, the dividing wall of hostility" (Eph. 2:14).

---

29   Filip Spagnoli, "Historical Overview of Violent Conflict," P.A.P.-BLOG // HUMAN RIGHTS ETC. (blog), http://filipspagnoli.wordpress.com/stats-on-human-rights/statistics-on-war-conflict/statistics-on-violent-conflict/, citing the New York Times, "Population Control, Marauder Style," November 6, 2011, http://www.nytimes.com/imagepages/2011/11/06/opinion/06atrocities_timeline.html?ref=Sunday.

But this is only half the story. Moses describes a characteristic of God we often forget: "The LORD is a warrior; the LORD is his name" (Exod. 15:3). And Solomon reminds us that there is a "time for war and a time for peace" (Eccles. 3:8).

Mankind does not experience world peace, because we do not have personal peace in our hearts. There can be no peace with man until we all find peace with God. Unfortunately, the book of Revelation warns us that this will not take place until Christ's return. If you don't believe it, all you have to do is look at how much time and money is now spent on personal security in our country. The evidence is all around us. We can safely say that all of mankind's efforts to bring world peace are simply not working. There is no doubt the world is getting worse. Although the economic bubble of the 1980's and 1990's gave many of us a false sense of security, the recent crises arising in several key areas of the world's economy show us just how close we are to a total breakdown.

It's into this world filled with selfishness and pride, a world fueled by envy and greed, that Jesus sends His followers with these challenging words: "Blessed are the peacemakers, for they will be called sons of God" (Matt. 5:9). He doesn't tell us to wait until everything gets better, nor does He ask us if we want to go. He simply says, "go and be a peacemaker."

In order to understand this Beatitude, we need to break it down into its central parts. This process begins with the word *peace*. If you ask most people to define the word *peace*, they would probably say something like "the absence of conflict." But this does not come close to capturing the depth of this biblical word.

Although many people have reached the conclusion that Jesus taught His followers to be pacifists, when you look at the full counsel of the Scriptures it is difficult to reach a consensus. When Jesus saw the wickedness of the moneychangers who were taking advantage of the poor who came to the temple to worship, He literally took up arms against them (a whip) and drove them out of the temple (John 2:15). Jesus' response to injustice was not what we would usually define as pacifism, but rather a form of righteous, yet violent, indignation. In his book entitled *My War*, Andy Rooney recalls his early experience as a pacifist. Rooney had believed the idea that any peace is better than any war. This did not hold up after WWII, when he entered the Buchenwald concentration camp. When Rooney saw the sheer horror of the atrocities that had been committed, he quickly realized that his pacifist theory was bankrupt. He says, "For the first time, I knew for certain that any peace is not better than any war."[30] A similar scenario caused Christian theologian Dietrich Bonhoeffer to go against his belief in pacifism and conclude that sometimes it is necessary to stand up and fight against evil. Bonhoeffer is quoted as saying, "Silence in the face of evil is itself evil: God will not hold us guiltless. Not to speak is to speak. Not to act is to act."[31] As the saying goes, some things are worth fighting for, and some things are worth fighting against.

One thing is for certain: Jesus never implied that the peace He gave His followers would keep them from experiencing violence

---

30   "A Review of Andy Rooney's *My War*", On Violence (blog), May 28, 2010, http://onviolence.com/?e=229.

31   Eric Metaxas, *Bonhoeffer: Pastor, Martyr, Prophet, Spy* (Nashville, TN: Thomas Nelson, 2010), backcover insert.

and opposition in this world. In fact, He said just the opposite. "I have said these things to you, that in me you may have peace. In the world you will have tribulation. But take heart; I have overcome the world" (John 16:33 ESV). In *The Message*, Eugene Peterson paraphrases this verse as follows: "I've told you all this so that trusting me, you will be unshakable and assured, deeply at peace. In this godless world you will continue to experience difficulties. But take heart! I've conquered the world" (John 16:33 MSG). It would appear that the peace Jesus is speaking of has very little to do with the conditions of outward conflict in the world around us, and everything to do with peace in our hearts.

THE MEANING OF SHALOM

The Hebrew word translated as "peace" in the Bible is the word *shalom*. *Shalom* is a broad term that covers a whole host of areas including, but not limited to, health, prosperity, harmony, and wholeness. It certainly implies more than the absence of hostility. According to one Bible scholar, "in at least two thirds of the biblical references, *shalom* indicates a total fulfillment that comes when individuals experience God's presence."[32] To wish somebody *shalom* is to wish them the full measure of God's power, presence, prosperity, and peace in their lives. This idea is clearly displayed in the blessing that Moses taught Aaron and his sons, "The LORD bless you and keep you; the LORD make his face shine upon you, and be gracious to you; the LORD turn his face toward you, and give you peace [Shalom]" (Num. 6:24–26). The study of the word *shalom* also takes us back a couple chapters to the idea of righteousness. An essential ingredient

---

32 "Jehovah Shalom, the Lord is Peace," accessed May 28, 2013, http://www.preceptaustin.org/jehovah_shalom_the_lord_is_peace.htm#shalom.

in biblical peace is the righteousness of God. When we hunger for God's righteousness, causing us to be in right relationship to God through the death and resurrection of Jesus, only then is lasting peace possible. There is no peace without the righteousness of God! Those who pursue peace must use righteousness as a guide.

The Greek word translated as "make" in the term *peacemakers* means to make, to cause, or to prepare. It requires action on the part of the person who is called a peacemaker.[33] This pretty much sums it up for us. Jesus wants us to get out there in this fallen world, a world where war, conflicts, and violence are common. But instead of focusing on these things, our job is to help make, cause, or maybe even prepare the soil, so that peace becomes possible: first with God, and then with men.

The Beatitude goes on to say "for they will be called sons of God." The Greek word translated as "called" literally means "to be officially given, or to bear a title."[34] This is the same idea that we might think of when a king or queen is crowned. This new official title becomes a primary identity. When people see us, their first thought should be, "there goes a son (or daughter) of God." The words "son of God" are quite significant here. The word *son* carried a lot of meaning in Jewish culture. The son received an inheritance. The son carried his father's name and quite often assumed his father's social rank. By calling us peacemakers, and tying that to the title of a son of God, Jesus is implying that our everyday lives should cause people to recognize us for who we legally are: sons

---

33   Bible Study Tools.com, New Testament Greek Lexicon, s.v. "poieo," http://www.biblestudytools.com/lexicons/greek/kjv/poieo.html.

34   Bible.org, NET Bible Study Environment Online, Greek word study ["Grk/Heb" tab] of Matthew 5:9, s.v. "will be called," accessed July 2013, https://net.bible.org/#!bible/Matthew+5.

of God, and legal heirs to His Kingdom. Our lives should help to bring God's Kingdom to bear, no matter what circumstances we find ourselves living in.

A good example can be seen in the life of William Wilberforce, who lived from 1759 to 1833. Wilberforce was an English politician who led the movement to abolish the slave trade. In 1785, he underwent a conversion experience and became an evangelical Christian. This transformation resulted in major changes to his lifestyle. Wilberforce also developed a lifelong concern for reform. In 1787, he proposed his first legislation to abolish the slave trade throughout the British Empire. It took thirty years until the passage of the Slave Trade Act of 1807. When he started his crusade, England was severely divided on the issue, and no one saw any way that the two sides would ever be brought together. Not only were the people divided over this issue, but so was the Anglican Church. This conflict became the perfect ground for Wilberforce to display his role as a peacemaker. Under Wilberforce's leadership, a group of men and women began meeting and praying together. People from different denominational backgrounds began to find common cause in Jesus Christ. In the end, as they worked together to fulfill one of the most basic tenets of the Gospel—the belief that all human beings have value and worth, which we see clearly displayed by Jesus' willingness to die for our sins—their unity helped to display, for all to see, the power of the Gospel to bring peace: first to individual hearts, and then to an entire nation. Only a true peacemaker, a "son of God," could be used to help do something like this in England.

In his second letter to the church at Corinth, Paul gives us a good working definition of what a peacemaker should look like:

> All this is from God, who reconciled us to himself through Christ and gave us the ministry of reconciliation: that God was reconciling the world to himself in Christ, not counting men's sins against them. And he has committed to us the message of reconciliation. We are therefore Christ's ambassadors, as though God were making his appeal through us. We implore you on Christ's behalf: Be reconciled to God. God made him who had no sin to be sin for us, so that in him we might become the righteousness of God. – 2 Cor. 5:18–21

Paul starts with personal reconciliation between God and us. The peace that both Jesus and Paul are concerned with is peace with God; our sins are forgiven and no longer counted against us. Now that this has been accomplished, Paul says we become ambassadors (which carries a similar meaning to *sons*, in that we become official representatives of God) whose job it is to help others become reconciled with God. The mandate is clear. As those who have already been reconciled through our relationship to Jesus Christ, we must take action. As peacemakers, we should be actively working to reconcile men to God and to one another. It must start in our homes and with our families, move out to our workplace and schools, our communities, and then ultimately to the ends of the earth.

When you take time to think about it, you realize that this is no easy task. And just in case we might start to feel overwhelmed by our responsibilities, Paul reminds us of an important truth: "If it is possible, as far as it depends on you, live at peace with everyone" (Rom. 12:18). We are not guaranteed success. The results are not always up to us. "As far as it is possible" we are to live at peace. But the implication in this text is that sometimes, and with some people, *shalom* is not possible. I'm going to be politically incorrect and just say it: some people are unpleasant to be around. They seem to find something to complain about all the time. They are often rude and crass, making everyone who comes around them uncomfortable. Peace may not be possible with such people. Our main responsibility in these types of situations is to make sure that we are not the problem, that the lack of peace is not starting with us.

TWO REWARDS FOR PEACEMAKERS

Because this job is so difficult, Jesus reminds us of two rewards tied to the role of peacemaker: blessing and sonship. As with all of the sayings in the Beatitudes, Jesus starts by reminding us there is a way of life, only available through a personal relationship with Him, that leads to a life of blessings. We know He's not talking about ease and comfort, but the presence and power of God, no matter what our circumstances are. We now also know that when He says we will be called sons of God, He is talking about a new family relationship, where we actually take on His family name. Let me share a personal illustration of why this is so important. My mom and dad are both musicians who have dedicated all of their professional lives to the field of music. From organists to professors to playing in symphony orchestras and accompanying musical productions, if there was a classical musical event, usually my parents were involved. Because of their willingness to work in this field, they are very well known in the greater Battle Creek, Michigan, area. When I became a financial advisor, I couldn't believe how often I would meet with people who knew my parents. "You're Dan and Emily's son," "Your parents are so talented," "What instrument do you play?" Even today, when I talk to people in Battle Creek, they sometimes refer to me as Dan and Emily's son. As their son, I am recognized by and carry their name.

But now I am grown. I have three children of my own (Daphne, Nate, and Ana). Two of my children are stepchildren, and one is my natural child. If you know Ana, you know that she not only looks like me, but she acts like me as well. She carries my DNA and bears my image wherever she goes. I feel really bad for her about that, but there is nothing I can do about it. But what is also amazing to see is that my older children, although not mine by birth, have become mine through relationship. As a result of this relationship, they too have begun to bear some of my image. And recently, Nate chose to legally take my family name as his own.

Do you see the ramifications here? In the same way that my children are called by my name, I am my Heavenly Father's son, called by His name. That's the incredible promise that Jesus is making to us here. When we become peacemakers, we will be recognized as sons (and daughters) of God. All around us is emptiness and pain. We don't have to look far to find broken families, feuding neighbors, alcohol and drug-addicted men and women, angry co-workers, etc. You and I are called to be peacemakers, bringing reconciliation into every one of these painful situations we encounter.

CONCLUSION

As we get ready to close this chapter, I want to return to a point we covered in the last chapter. The key to success with this Beatitude is having the right fuel motivating us. Am I so grateful for the *shalom* I have received through Jesus Christ that I am willing to stay in the battle, even if there is a personal cost? The bottom line is this: peace usually comes at a cost. It's so much easier just to walk away from a problem than it is to get involved. I have enough stress in my life already, why look for more? Another challenge comes when the very people we are trying to help, turn on us. Without a fresh experience of God's mercy raining down on our lives and without the purity of heart to see God working in the world around us, it will be impossible to fulfill this call. If you try to do this in your own strength, and by your own resources, you will fail! But when we remember whose name we now carry, and the price that was paid for us to receive it, the supernatural power of God starts working through us, enabling ordinary people like you and me to do things that we would never be able to do on our own.

For over two thousand years, a vast army of peacemakers has been living out this truth. Reconciled to God, they have been able to love the unlovely, care for the outcasts, touch the untouchables, bring down unjust laws, and bring peace to those who were at war with God, all through the power of the Holy Spirit.

CHALLENGE

I want to challenge you to take the time to pray and ask God how well you are bearing His Name. Ask Him to reveal which areas of your life are getting in the way of your role as a peacemaker. As a Christian, this is not an optional role you can choose. This is how the world will recognize that you are obeying God. It is my prayer that Christians everywhere will wake up from their slumber and embrace the calling given them by our Master: "*Blessed are the peacemakers, for they will be called sons of God.*"

GOING DEEPER

1) How might you have defined the word *peace* before reading this chapter?

2) Has that definition changed?

3) In your own words, describe the role of a peacemaker.

4) Pray and ask God to give you specific people or circumstances where you can begin to bring peace. (Pray through your family, your co-workers, fellow students, neighbors, friends, homeless people you see on the streets, etc.)

5) Commit to memorizing 2 Corinthians 5:18–21. (If you're new to Scripture memorization, focus on one verse at a time so you don't get overwhelmed.)

CHAPTER 9

THE BLESSING OF PERSECUTION

Blessed are those who are persecuted because of righteousness,
for theirs is the kingdom of heaven.

Matthew 5:10

IN THIS CHAPTER, WE COME to the Beatitude that most people like to forget. It presents a truth, that, if we're honest, we'd just rather not think about. Listen to Jesus' words here: "Blessed are those who are persecuted because of righteousness, for theirs is the kingdom of heaven. Blessed are you when people insult you, persecute you and falsely say all kinds of evil against you because of me. Rejoice and be glad, because great is your reward in heaven, for in the same way they persecuted the prophets who were before you" (Matt. 5:10–12). There is something about the word *"persecution."* Just saying it evokes images of pain and suffering. My mind immediately goes to scenes from the movies I've seen where men and women are burned at the stake. I think of the stories I've read of mothers having their babies killed right before their eyes. I also think of stories like Daniel, where his faith caused him to be thrown to the lions, the early Christians who faced this same type of persecution in the Roman Coliseum, and of course the brave pastors who suffered torture instead of renouncing their faith—men like Richard Wurmbrand and Dietrich Bonhoeffer. We know these things happened in the past, but surely they don't take place in our enlightened world today?

Then we read a story about someone like Iranian pastor Youcef Nadarkhani. As of this writing in 2013, for most of the past three years pastor Nadarkhani was incarcerated in an Iranian prison. Every day, pastor Nadarkhani was faced with the threat of execution. What were his crimes? He was charged with abandoning Islam and refusing to renounce his Christian faith. This 37-year-old husband and father of two spent almost 1,100 days in isolation and torture. Over that time he had very little opportunity to see his wife, his two sons, or his church members. Unable to break Youcef's faith in Jesus Christ, the Iranian authorities at one point also arrested his wife. They even threatened to give his children to a strict Muslim family, to be raised in the doctrines of the Islamic faith. We can imagine the emotional pain and terrible anxiety that Youcef and his wife and family suffered as a result of all this persecution, yet—if we are to take our Lord's words in this text seriously—then we would have to say that they were actually blessed.

A couple of years ago one of my fellow elders told me about attending a meeting of middle school teachers, which was supposed to cover topics dealing with how to teach children about important issues having to do with their health. The room was packed with both teachers and parents. The topic of how to teach homosexuality in a classroom setting became the main focus of the meeting. My friend was never threatened with prison or openly persecuted, but when he stood up and shared his views, the tension in the room became evident. Several people suggested that his views were ignorant, and that he should keep them to himself. The very people who have redefined the word *tolerance* to mean "accepting all viewpoints as equally valid," were, by their own definition, being intolerant of my friend's Christian worldview. In essence, he was singled out and insulted for standing up for what he sincerely believes as a Christian. And whether it involves a physical threat to our bodies or a public ridicule of our beliefs, the question remains: are we really blessed when this happens?

THE BLESSING OF PERSECUTION

In order to answer that question, we need to wrestle with what Jesus actually means in this text. One of the first things I want you to notice is the way Jesus moves from a general statement in verse 10, "blessed are those," to a very personal statement in verse 11, "blessed are you." Many Bible commentators agree that this shift was made to emphasize a very important point: as a Christian, persecution is not only a possibility, but a certainty to all who truly desire to follow our Lord. Listen to Paul's words in 2 Timothy: "In fact, everyone who wants to live a godly life in Christ Jesus will be persecuted" (2 Tim. 3:12). If it wasn't already clear, it should be now. Persecution is a normal and expected part of the Christian life.

So let's return to our text. What does Jesus mean when he says, "Blessed are you when people insult you, persecute you and falsely say all kinds of evil against you because of me" (Matt. 5:11)? A helpful tool in figuring out what Jesus actually means is to eliminate the things we know He doesn't mean. Have you heard of a bucket list? A bucket list is a list of the most important things you want to do before you die (kick the bucket). For some people it might mean a trip to see the Swiss Alps, to bungee jump on their fiftieth birthday, take time to watch a major league baseball game in every stadium in America, or even run with the bulls in Pamplona, Spain. But when Jesus says, "Blessed are those who are persecuted," He's not telling us to run out and make sure we find persecution before we die. This is not a new item to add to your bucket list. So don't think I'm going to spend this chapter telling you how you can find persecution, because I'm not. Jesus' message is much simpler than that. As Christians we don't need to go looking for persecution, because when we live a life reflecting the righteousness of Christ, persecution will come and find us. We are forewarned in Scripture:

> All men will hate you because of me, but he who stands firm to the end will be saved. – Matt. 10:22

> Remember the words I spoke to you: "No servant is greater than his master." If they persecuted me, they will persecute you also. – John 15:20a

> I have told you these things, so that in me you may have peace. In this world you will have trouble. But take heart! I have overcome the world. – John 16:33

> For it has been granted to you on behalf of Christ not only to believe on him, but also to suffer for him. – Phil. 1:29

THE BATTLE BETWEEN DARKNESS AND LIGHT

As disciples of Jesus Christ, we are called to help bring His Kingdom to bear here on earth. But unless we understand there are two conflicting Kingdoms at work here, we will never be able to grasp the nature of the battle into which we have entered. Movies such as *Star Wars*, *The Lord of the Rings*, and *The Matrix* give us an idea of this cosmic battle between the forces of Light and the forces of Darkness. These stories resonate with our hearts because they point us toward a deeper truth; there is an actual battle, raging right here on earth, and it is every bit as vicious as anything displayed in these movies. When we become disciples of our Lord, we enter the battle on the side of the kingdom of Light. But this world is (temporarily) under the influence of the kingdom of Darkness. Listen to how Paul describes unbelievers in the second book he wrote to the church at Corinth: "The god of this age has blinded the minds of unbelievers, so that they cannot see the light of the gospel that displays the glory of Christ, who is the image of God" (2 Cor. 4:4). Did you catch what he said? The minds of unbelievers are blinded to the truth of Jesus Christ. So when people around us stand opposed to what we believe, it should not catch us by surprise or make us hate or despise them. They are simply doing what lost people do.

So Jesus isn't saying that we should go looking for persecution. But he is warning us that we will experience it as a member of His Kingdom. He even goes on to tell us why. He says it will be "because of righteousness." When we begin to reflect the righteousness of Christ (as we talked about back in chapter five), this dark world cannot put up with it for very long. Although we will have wonderful opportunities to minister to people who are broken and lost, some will not only reject our message, but also openly oppose our right to share it. Not only that, Jesus goes on to tell us they will say false things about us. Isn't that exactly what we see with the false witnesses who lied about Jesus at His trial before the Sanhedrin? He tells us plainly in John 15: "If they persecuted me, they will persecute you also" (John 15:20).

Do you know what the hardest part of being persecuted for Jesus' sake actually is? It is that the world will not admit that your actions are righteous. They will take the things you do and twist the truth, making your good and loving actions look evil and intolerant. They won't accuse you of being righteous, but just the opposite. They'll paint your righteous acts as wanton wickedness. We see this in the way the media covers issues such as abortion and same-sex marriage. Even though many Christians stand up in love to support the sanctity of life and to defend the biblical definition of marriage, the press often dismisses their Scripture-based argument as mean-spirited, ridiculous, and hopelessly out of touch. Anyone who uses the Bible as a reference for what they believe is labeled as ignorant, illiterate, and intolerant. New words have been constructed, such as "homophobic," in an attempt to frame Christians as hateful and bigoted. But this should not surprise us. They did the same thing to the early church. Those faithful Christian men and women were accused of committing incest because they talked about loving their brothers and sisters. They were charged with being atheists because they refused to worship idols. They were even charged as enemies of the state because they would not swear allegiance to Caesar over Jesus Christ.

When you or I are persecuted for our faith, the charge will always be something else. You won't be charged with being too righteous. Instead you will be accused of being intolerant, bigoted, or even hateful. But this should never stop us; it should strengthen us. Our hearts should grow bolder when we realize that the persecution is actually a sign that we are "on mission" with our Lord. It is also a sign that the transformation promised at our new birth is actually taking place. We are beginning to reflect the light of Jesus Christ to a dark and broken world. And because their "minds are blinded," the light hurts their eyes. Of course, the key here is to stand up for the truth in love. That's why the lessons of meekness, righteousness, mercy, purity of heart, and peacemaking are so important in preparing us for this challenge. If our hearts are not broken for those blind people lost in sin, if we aren't concerned for the eternal destiny of those we encounter, then we have the wrong motives for what we are doing.

We see clearly now why Jesus chose to connect righteousness with persecution. In fact, the very world Jesus came to save . . . crucified Him because of His righteousness. So we shouldn't expect it to put up with our righteousness, either. And this leads us to another important insight. If you're not beginning to reflect the character and nature of our God in your daily walk, you probably won't be persecuted. Listen to this quote from a pastor named Ajith Fernando, who is from the country of Sri Lanka:

> In a world where physical health, appearance, and convenience have gained almost idolatrous prominence, God may be calling Christians to demonstrate the glory of the gospel by being joyful and content while enduring pain and

hardship. People who are unfulfilled after pursuing things that do not satisfy may be astonished to see Christians who are joyful and content after depriving themselves for the gospel. This may be a new way to demonstrate the glory of the gospel to this hedonistic culture.

I have a great fear for the church. The West is fast becoming an unreached region. The Bible and history show that suffering is an essential ingredient in reaching unreached people. Will the loss of a theology of suffering lead the Western church to become ineffective in evangelism? The church in the East is growing, and because of that God's servants are suffering. Significant funding and education come to the East from the West. With funding and education comes influence. Could Westerners influence Eastern Christians to abandon the Cross by communicating that they must be doing something wrong if they suffer in this way? Christians in both the East and the West need to have a firm theology of suffering if they are to be healthy and bear fruit.[35]

These words should rock us to our very core. Are we guilty of forgetting the cross? Do we try to minimize the suffering involved in the Christian life? These questions require deep reflection on our parts. Life as a Christian in modern America does not entail the same level of physical suffering as is experienced by many Christians in Africa, Asia, and the Middle East.

---

35   Tim Stafford, "Ajith Fernando: On the Anvil of Suffering," Christianity Today (October 2012): accessed June 5, 2013, http://www.christianitytoday.com/ct/2012/october/the-choice.html.

However, Jesus makes it clear that suffering is to be expected. It might take the form of workplace intimidation (either embrace the new ideologies or lose your position); it could come as Christian ethics are marginalized through legislation (literally outlawing a pastor's right to speak biblically concerning certain social issues); it could even come through the restriction of who is eligible to homeschool (deeming Christian parents as unfit to teach their children.) You may think these examples are a stretch. But they're not. This sort of intimidation is happening all around us. The more we reflect the true character and nature of our Lord, the more likely it is that we'll experience this persecution ourselves. And according to Jesus, we should consider ourselves blessed! The kingdom of this world is in an all-out war against the kingdom of Light. These types of battles are going to continue, and most likely escalate, until our Lord returns. We don't really have a choice. If we are to follow our Lord's teachings (teachings that this world rejects), the persecution is going to come. Our main responsibility is not to try to avoid persecution, but to honor our Lord. Jesus is telling us as plainly as He can that we can be blessed even, and especially, when we are persecuted.

THE REWARD

In order to help motivate His followers, Jesus points us toward a future reward; He even calls the reward "great." If you're like me, you may be wondering at this point: "Is it really possible to live this way? How can I face suffering and still believe that I am blessed? Who in their right mind would rejoice when they were persecuted for Jesus' name?" Allow me to share a personal experience. I remember hiking with my wife, Sonia, at the Sleeping Bear Dunes National

Park (located along the beautiful shores of Lake Michigan) about twelve years ago. There are several trails that hikers can choose from, many of which are very physically challenging. One of the trails is 1.75 miles long. It's made up of several steep inclines and declines, made even more difficult because of the sand. The day we went the temperature was over ninety, and there were warnings posted about the danger of dehydration and sun poisoning. We set out with several other people, all in good spirits. As the physical stress of the journey began to wear people down, many decided to turn back. I remember Sonia and I asking ourselves several times, "Is this worth it?" When we finally came over the last dune and saw the sparkling blue water below, we actually became giddy. We ran down and plunged in. The water was so cold that my body started giving off little trails of steam. We laughed and played in that water for several minutes. Finally, Sonia looked at me and said, "I wonder if this is what heaven is like?" The pleasure of that moment is still vivid in both of our memories to this very day. The reward for our perseverance was incredible. But if we had given up and quit anywhere along the way, surrendering to the hardship and pain, we would have missed the awesome gift that God had waiting for us at the finish line. Those who turned back never got to experience what we did that day.

Now listen to this description of the cost of discipleship, from German theologian (and Christian martyr) Dietrich Bonhoeffer:

> The messengers of Jesus will be hated to the end of time. They will be blamed for all the division, which rend cities and homes. Jesus and his disciples will be condemned on all sides for undermining family life, and for leading the

nation astray; they will be called crazy fanatics and disturbers of the peace. The disciples will be sorely tempted to desert their Lord. But the end is also near, and they must hold on and persevere until it comes. Only he will be blessed who remains loyal to Jesus and his word until the end.[36]

This is what Jesus is saying to us in Matthew 5:10. "Yes, I know I'm calling you to a journey that is long and difficult. I know that you will experience suffering, persecution, and pain along the way. But if you will hang on to the end, the reward is so much greater than you can now imagine." The bottom line is this: Jesus is promising His people that there is something out there in the future, a supernatural reward, that is much more valuable than a persecution-free life here on earth.

The author of Hebrews reminds us that Jesus used this same motivation to give himself strength as He faced the cross: "Jesus . . . *who for the joy that was set before Him endured the cross*, despising the shame, and has sat down at the right hand of the throne of God" (Heb. 12:2 NKJV; italics mine). In 1 Corinthians, Paul uses similar imagery by comparing the rigors of the Christian life to an athlete running in a race: "Do you not know that those who run in a race all run, but one receives the prize? Run in such a way that you may obtain it. And everyone who competes for the prize is temperate in all things. Now they do it to obtain a perishable crown, but we for an imperishable crown" (1 Cor. 9:24–25 NKJV).

Why would anyone embrace such a life? We will only do so when we understand that there is a great payoff waiting for us at

---

36   Dietrich Bonhoeffer, *The Cost of Discipleship* (New York: Touchstone, 1937), 239.

the finish line. Once we know we have more to gain than lose, we can honestly say we're blessed even when we're persecuted. There is nothing in this world that isn't worth giving up, when compared to the things that we will receive as part of our inheritance in God's Kingdom.

Richard Wurmbrand had this to say about his experience of persecution in a Romanian prison: "It was strictly forbidden to preach to other prisoners. It was understood that whoever was caught doing this received a severe beating. A number of us decided to pay the price for the privilege of preaching, so we accepted their [the communists'] terms. It was a deal; we preached and they beat us. We were happy preaching. They were happy beating us, so everyone was happy."[37]

Hugh Latimer was burned at the stake in 1555 because he refused to accept many of the teachings of the Catholic Church, which he saw as unbiblical. Here is a quote of what he said to his friend Nicholas Ridley as they stood tied to the stakes and were about to die: "Be of good comfort, Mr. Ridley, and play the man! We shall this day light such a candle by God's grace, in England, as I trust never shall be put out."[38] Here is someone who understood Jesus' meaning when He said, "Rejoice and be glad, because great is your reward in heaven" (Matt. 5: 12a). No matter what we face now, like Hugh Latimer, we can rejoice in looking forward to Jesus' promise of a future reward.

---

37   Richard Wurmbrand, *Tortured For Christ* (Bartlesville, OK: Living Sacrifice, 1967), quoted on http://updates.theworldrace.org/?filename=pick-up-the-torch-romania.

38   F. L. Cross and E. A. Livingstone, ed., The Oxford Dictionary of the Christian Church, 2nd ed. (Oxford: Oxford University Press, 1997), s.vv. "Latimer, Hugh," "Ridley, Nicholas".

Just in case that's not enough motivation, Jesus also points us to the multitude of faithful saints who have gone before us. Look closely at the second half of verse 12, "Rejoice and be glad, because great is your reward in heaven, *for in the same way they persecuted the prophets who were before you*" (Matt. 5:12; italics mine). When we suffer for Jesus Christ, our names are added to a long list of faithful servants who willingly put the kingdom of God over personal comfort or gain. These men and women risked everything for the cause of Christ. Many of them are listed in Hebrews 11, which is often referred to as the "Faith Hall of Fame." Much like a baseball player whose faithfulness and perseverance lands them a spot in Cooperstown (the location of professional baseball's Hall of Fame), this famous list reminds us that God honors believers who stay the course and finish the race, especially in the face of persecution. In chapter 12, the author of Hebrews illustrates the close connection between all of God's suffering saints throughout the church age:

> Therefore, *since we are surrounded by such a great cloud of witnesses*, let us throw off everything that hinders and the sin that so easily entangles. And let us run with perseverance the race marked out for us, [2] fixing our eyes on Jesus, the pioneer and perfecter of faith. For the joy set before him he endured the cross, scorning its shame, and sat down at the right hand of the throne of God. [3] Consider him who endured such opposition from sinners, so that you will not grow weary and lose heart. – Heb. 12:1–3 (italics mine)

Picture the finish of the marathon race at the Olympics. The bleachers in the coliseum are full to capacity (*a great cloud of witnesses*). The crowd roars in anticipation as the runners enter the stadium for the last lap. When the runners start their final kick, the crowd jumps to its feet to cheer them on. This is the picture we receive here in this text. Those great men and women of God, who have suffered persecution and persevered, are cheering us on, eagerly waiting for us to realize our great reward!

The apostle Paul, who arguably suffered as much as any follower in the history of the Church, describes how the persecution and suffering pale in comparison to the rewards of obedience to Christ's call:

> But whatever were gains to me I now consider loss for the sake of Christ. What is more, I consider everything a loss because of the surpassing worth of knowing Christ Jesus my Lord, for whose sake I have lost all things. I consider them garbage, that I may gain Christ and be found in him, not having a righteousness of my own that comes from the law, but that which is through faith in Christ—the righteousness that comes from God on the basis of faith. I want to know Christ—yes, to know the power of his resurrection and participation in his sufferings, becoming like him in his death, and so, somehow, attaining to the resurrection from the dead.

> Not that I have already obtained all this, or have already arrived at my goal, but I press on to take hold of that for which Christ Jesus took hold of me. Brothers and sisters, I do not consider myself yet to have taken hold of it. But one thing I do: Forgetting what is behind and straining

toward what is ahead, I press on toward the goal to win
the prize for which God has called me heavenward in
Christ Jesus. – Phil. 4:7–14

Paul indicates that the greatest reward of all is the increased
depth of his relationship to the Lord as a result of his suffering.
We see this same sentiment expressed in the famous quote from
Jim Elliot, a missionary martyred in Ecuador: "He is no fool who
gives up what he cannot keep to obtain that which he cannot lose."
When we see what Jesus did for us, we know that it's more than
worth it to suffer for his sake. I don't wish suffering on anyone. I
certainly don't wish it for myself. But it is part of what it means to
be a follower of Jesus Christ, especially as we begin to experience
the transformation that Jesus describes in the Beatitudes.

When we're set free from our old lives of emptiness and sin,
delivered from the misery of selfishness and pride, as we begin to
experience the cure for our broken spiritual condition, Jesus promises us a new life and a new experience of hope. He doesn't do this,
however, just so we can keep it to ourselves. As we'll see in the next
chapter, His purpose is so much greater than we could have ever
imagined: we are saved so we can go out into this lost and broken
world, acting as His agents of "salt and light" (Matt. 5:13–14).

The warning in this Beatitude is crystal clear: not everyone
will be excited about the new life you have found. If you take seriously the call to act as salt and light, you will face opposition. Some
people will think you are crazy and dismiss your actions as foolish;
others will be offended and push you away. But at some point in
time, you will face someone who is openly hostile. In each and
every one of these situations, Jesus' message is the same: "Don't be

surprised by persecution; you should expect it! Prepare your heart to persevere through it!" After all, following Jesus is costly, but the cost is nothing when you compare it to your eternal reward. "Blessed are those who are persecuted because of righteousness, for theirs is the kingdom of heaven" (Matt. 5:10).

GOING DEEPER

★Reread Matthew 5:10–12 and then answer these questions:

1) Up until this point, how have you viewed the idea of facing persecution?

2) How has reading this chapter affected your view?

3) How might the other Beatitudes prepare your heart for the intensity of the battle we face as Christians trying to follow Jesus in a fallen world?

4) Does it surprise you to know that right now, in several parts of the world, the persecution of Christians is at some of the highest levels in history?

5) How has following Jesus caused you to experience persecution?

CHAPTER 10

SALT AND LIGHT

You are the salt of the earth . . . You are the light of the world.

Matthew 5:13a, 14a

INFLUENTIAL PEOPLE

WHEN I WAS A KID, I used to love the colorful comics section in the Sunday morning newspaper. My favorite comic strip was called *Peanuts*, and it included the wonderful characters Charlie Brown, Lucy, Linus, Peppermint Patty, and of course, Snoopy. On one occasion, Peppermint Patty was talking to Charlie Brown as they walked home from school. The dialogue went something like this: "Guess what, Chuck? It's the first day of school and I already got sent to the principal's office. It was all your fault." Charlie replied, "My fault? How could it be my fault? Why do you say everything is my fault?" In response, Peppermint Patty said, "You're my friend, aren't you, Chuck? You should have been a better influence on me." While it's clear that Peppermint Patty was looking for a scapegoat, she may have actually been on to an important biblical principle: As followers of Jesus Christ, as people who have had our lives radically changed by our relationship to our Lord, we should be a good influence on our friends and family.

One thing I have stressed repeatedly throughout this book is Jesus' emphasis on the transformation that should be evident in the hearts of those who follow Him. He has clearly laid out the type of characteristics that ought to be manifested, as believers experience the life changes He promises. When these changes take place, when we surrender control of our hearts and minds to Jesus Christ, we begin to reflect the very character and nature of God. One of the most amazing things about God's plan for redeeming a lost world is the fact that He chooses to use people like you and me. We get to serve on the front lines in the battle to reach the souls who are going to be saved! There is no doubt that Peppermint Patty was onto something important for us to understand as Christians: we all have an influence on the people God places in our lives.

The question for you to wrestle with as you finish reading this book is important: What type of influence will you have? Will your walk with God be characterized by the principles we have discussed so far in this book: poverty of spirit, mourning over your sin, the meekness to surrender control of your life to God, a hunger for righteousness, showing the same mercy you have received, purity of heart, a willingness to share God's peace, and the faith to endure the world's persecution? Are you ready to admit that—apart from God—you are spiritually dead? Do you understand that you bring nothing to the table but a willing heart? Are you ready to accept God's diagnosis that you have a terminal disease, a disease that causes death in one hundred percent of the human race? Your only hope is to find the cure—acceptance of your condition, the humility to swallow your pride, and the willingness to accept God's offer of new life through Jesus Christ. This new life will take you through every step we just covered, in order to prepare you for service in God's Kingdom.

In Matthew 5:13–16, Jesus uses two powerful metaphors to help us understand what this new life of service in His Kingdom should look like. He compares his followers to salt and light. Take a few minutes to digest His words:

> You are the salt of the earth; but if the salt loses its flavor, how shall it be seasoned? It is then good for nothing but to be thrown out and trampled underfoot by men. You are the light of the world. A city that is set on a hill cannot be hidden. Nor do they light a lamp and put it under a basket, but on a lampstand, and it gives light to all who are in the house. Let your light so shine before men, that they may see your good works and glorify your Father in heaven. – Matt. 5:13–16 NKJV

Interestingly, Jesus does not give us a precise explanation of the word-picture of salt that He uses in this verse. Unlike verses 15 and 16, where he takes the time to explain what he wants us to understand about being the light which He references in verse 14, in this case he leaves it up to His followers to look for an understanding of His metaphor. We are to think through the ways salt is used in the world around us, and then apply those principles to His teaching. So our goal in this section is an important one—to try to understand the following question: "What exactly are the characteristics of salt that Jesus wants His followers to emulate?"

THE CHARACTERISTICS OF SALT

I don't know about you, but when I think of salt, I don't think of anything that's all that special. Pretty much like everyone else, I usually put a little bit on my food, but maybe because so much of what we eat already includes high levels of salt, I don't really appreciate its value. However, when we begin to study the characteristics of salt, along with its uses in Jesus' day, we see just how important it actually is to human life. In fact, throughout human history, because it is so vital for life and because it was not easily available everywhere, salt has been one of the most sought after elements on earth, along with gold. Although the list of its uses and benefits is very extensive, let's focus on five key characteristics of salt that can help us understand both the beauty and the depth of Jesus' challenge.

1) SALT HAS GREAT VALUE AND WORTH

Jesus referred to the motley group of followers who became His disciples as "salt." These men and women were not formally educated, and certainly not highly respected members of Jewish society. But when we understand just how valuable salt was in Jesus' day, this statement takes on new meaning. Salt was an absolute necessity of life in ancient times. In fact, it had so many uses that it was an acceptable substitute for money! It was not uncommon for the Roman army to use salt as a form of currency. Our word *salary* omes from the Latin word *salarium*, which referred to payments of salt given to the soldiers. We still use the phrase when we say that someone either is or is not "worth their salt."

We don't tend to think much about salt today, because we can get as much of it in pure form as we want. It's just that little bottle, with holes in the top, that sits on every table; right? But just imagine if salt were the only way you could keep your food from going bad, and if it were so valuable that people used it as money: that would change things, wouldn't it? Have you ever eaten white rice that hadn't had salt added to it? Throughout much of history and even in a great portion of the world still today, rice is the staple food source. It is consumed three times a day: for breakfast, lunch, and dinner. In Central and South America, corn meal (in the form of tortillas) plays a similar role. But without salt, rice and corn meal have a very bland flavor. Simply by adding salt, though, a monotonous meal becomes not only palatable, but even enjoyable. When my family and I lived in Guatemala, it always amazed me how creative the indigenous people could be when preparing their tortillas for a meal. They would add fresh avocado, squeeze in fresh lemon juice, and top it off with a sprinkle of salt before taking a bite. At first I didn't understand this process. But once I tried a tortilla prepared this way, I quickly became a fan. In Job 6:6 we read, "Is tasteless food eaten without salt, or is there flavor in the white of an egg?" Certainly, this reason alone gives salt great value and worth, and by implication, Jesus is saying, "You also have great value and worth."

2) SALT IS A POWERFUL PRESERVATIVE

Because there were very few ways to provide refrigeration in Jesus' day, salt was the primary source of food preservation. When thoroughly rubbed into meat before its storage, salt slows and sometimes even stops the process of decay. Think about the implications of that to our Christian lives. We are both personally, and collectively as the Church, given the task of helping Jesus to slow down, and in some cases even put a stop to, the decay in the world around us.

When we look at world history, even with all her faults, the Church of Jesus Christ has had a profoundly positive effect on the world. The dramatic impact of Jesus' followers starts with the uniquely Christian view that every human life has dignity and value. Prior to the birth of Christianity, women and children were considered to be of little or no value, women's equality was unheard of, and infanticide was a common practice.

This idea of human value can also be seen through the history of the Church's display of compassion for our fellow human beings. No other world religion has even come close to Christianity in this area. Hospitals as we now know them began because of compassionate Christians. The same is true with charities: the Red Cross, the Salvation Army, Goodwill, and many others were all started by faithful Christians trying to live out Jesus' commands. On top of that, most of the colleges and universities in the United States have Christian origins and were founded for Christian purposes. For a more detailed account of the incredible number of ways that the Church has acted as a preservative in society, I recommend the book *What If Jesus Had Never Been Born*, by the late Dr. D. James Kennedy.[39]

And still today our Lord calls us to be this type of positive benefit to the world in which we live. As Christ's followers, we are to serve as a type of moral antiseptic, helping to hold back the tide of evil and moral decay that is constantly rising up in a society composed of sinful men and women. We are to do this first by our actions—by how we live our lives and treat our neighbors; and then by our words—standing up for biblical principles and ideals. But

---

39   Kennedy, D. James. *What If Jesus Had Never Been Born* (Nashville: Nelson, 1994).

when we look around at the state of the Christian Church in the Western world today, we have to ask ourselves how well we are fulfilling our role as salt. What preserving effects are we having on our culture? Are we helping to hold back moral decay? Sadly, at least in America and Western Europe, the honest answer is probably: not nearly enough. When Christians are abandoning their spouses, cheating their employers, and watching filth on television at the same statistical level as their non-believing neighbors, there is a problem. In many areas, the Church has lost its saltiness.

There is an interesting text in 2 Thessalonians. "For the secret power of lawlessness is already at work; but the one who now holds it back will continue to do so till he is taken out of the way" (2 Thess. 2:7). Regardless of your interpretation of end time events, this Scripture points to the fact that it is God's Spirit working through God's people that holds back the power of darkness, keeping it from completely overwhelming this world.

In the same way that salt preserves and stops food from spoiling, Jesus says to His followers, "You are to do the same thing in this world. You are to be that special ingredient that preserves your society from complete corruption. You are to help preserve it from total decay!" As Christians we need to remember an important truth: no matter how advanced our technology becomes, there always lies within the human heart the seed of its own demise. An honest review of human history reveals the intrinsic weakness of our fallen human nature. Humankind, apart from God and left to our own devices, will always self-destruct. It doesn't matter when or where a civilization has arisen and gained a period of influence over the earth, there has always come a decline from the height of purity, often even to the point of final collapse. While man in his greatest moments may act generously and compassionately toward his neighbors, even the best of intentions and the noblest of people can become selfish and self-serving: the lure of power, pleasure, and money is just too great. As Phillip Keller reminds us, "Only the restraining influence of the presence of God in a person's life can counteract this drift downward. Only the total transformation of human character can slow the sure slide into subversive and destructive life styles."[40]

3) SALT PROMOTES HEALING

Believe it or not, in Christ's day salt was one of the primary forms of medication. Unlike our modern world, in the first century there were no national chain pharmacies such as CVS or Rite Aid standing on every street corner. The common medications that we take for granted today, such as aspirin and antibiotics, were simply not known back then. In Jesus's day, the majority of medications were a mixture of specialty herbs, but of all the common household treatments used, salt was by far the most versatile. It was recognized for its sterilizing properties, and so was used to help prevent the spread of infection in wounds. When someone was injured in battle, or a shepherd was bitten by a predator, or a child was scraped up in a fall, a strong solution of salt water was used to clean and sterilize the wound.

Jesus understood the healing power of salt, so when He told His disciples that they were the salt of the earth, He most certainly

---

40   Keller, *Salt*, 101.

had healing in mind, as well as preservation. The Old Testament prophets foretold a day when the Messiah would come bringing healing to the sick and mending to the broken hearted. Listen to the words of Isaiah: "The Spirit of the Sovereign Lord is on me, because the Lord has anointed me to preach good news to the poor. He has sent me to bind up the brokenhearted, to proclaim freedom for the captives and release from darkness for the prisoners" (Isaiah 61:1). In Luke chapter 4, Jesus reads this very quote from Isaiah and then says, "Today this scripture is fulfilled in your hearing" (Luke 4:21). Jesus' life was a wonderful fulfillment of this prophesy. Everything that Jesus did literally brought health and wholeness to the people He encountered. Jesus' command to His followers was to imitate what they saw in Him. In the same way that Jesus sent His disciples out into the world to help the sick and suffering, Jesus is calling us today to do the same.

As we have said many times throughout this book, we have a society that is suffering from terminal illness. And yet amid all of its maladies, we are called to make a contribution that will help in its recovery!

4) SALT CAN LOSE ITS USEFULNESS

Look back at our text, "You are the salt of the earth. But if the salt loses its saltiness, how can it be made salty again? It is no longer good for anything, except to be thrown out and trampled by men" (Matt. 5:13). Jesus says that if salt loses its flavor, it is worthless. Now technically speaking, salt cannot lose its saltiness; sodium chloride is a stable compound. But in the part of the world where Jesus lived, salt was collected from around the Dead Sea. Due to the nature of the work required to gather the salt, the crystals were often contaminated with other minerals, because the salt formations in this area were full of impurities. When it rained, it was possible for the rain to wash out the salt and its saltiness, making what remained of no value. The remains would still look like salt, but they would have none of the positive qualities we have discussed. Think about the ramifications of that point: in your Christian life, the incredible transformation you experienced at your new birth can be slowly drained of its power. When the thinking and values of this world replace a biblical worldview, the heart becomes hard and lifeless.

Amazingly, even after it loses its purity and flavor, salt maintains its ability to destroy vegetation. One of the cruelest punishments that kings used to pronounce over the people they conquered was the decree to salt the land. When this was done, the land could no longer produce crops to feed the people. Simply by applying salt to the earth, whole areas of ground would become worthless tracts of land, absolutely devoid of life and good for nothing.

Again, it's easy to see the spiritual ramifications of this principle. There is nothing more powerful for bringing health and healing to our world than the Spirit of God working through the transformed heart of one of God's people. Conversely, there is also nothing more damaging to the cause of Christ than a marginal Christian, professing faith while living like everyone else in the world. Mahatma Gandhi is famously quoted as saying, "I like your Christ, I do not like your Christians. Your Christians are so unlike your Christ."[41]

---

41   Mahatma Gandhi, Quote Data Base, http://www.quotedb.com/quotes/1905.

5) SALT HAS TO BE APPLIED TO WORK

Salt cannot add flavor to food, it cannot bring healing to the injured, nor can it act as a preservative, if it is left sitting in the cupboard. To be effective it has to be applied. As believers, we cannot hide ourselves away from the pain and brokenness we see in the world around us. We cannot make Jesus look more attractive if we opt out of our society. We must be able to mix with the world in which we live, without becoming like the world. As mentioned above, whenever the church has actively engaged in the culture, acting as salt in order to flavor, heal, and preserve, the results have been life-changing!

THE LIGHT OF THE WORLD

The second word picture Jesus used about His followers was "light." In this illustration, He gives us a much clearer picture of what He means:

> You are the light of the world. A city on a hill cannot be hidden. Neither do people light a lamp and put it under a bowl. Instead they put it on its stand, and it gives light to everyone in the house. In the same way, let your light shine before men, that they may see your good deeds and praise your Father in heaven. – Matt. 5:14–16

In this text, to be the light of the world means to illuminate the darkness so that others can see reality. One of the most frightening things in the world is to be alone in the dark. Have you ever lain awake in bed trying to go to sleep? All of a sudden you hear a creak or a bang. You try to see, but the darkness robs you of sight. You can occasionally make out vague shapes or objects, but you can't be sure of what you see. Darkness distorts reality. Everything looks different in the dark. It is only when you turn on the light that you see things as they really are.

Notice the simple application in verse 16, "Let your light shine before men." The key is at the end of the verse—"before men." You can turn on a light in an empty room and it will overcome the darkness. But if the room is empty, no one will see. In the same way, you can live the Christian life in isolation, locking yourself away from a world in need. But when you do, no one is helped. If you want your light to shine, it needs to shine before men. Somebody must be able to see what God is doing in and through your life, if it's going to make a difference in this world.

TWO EFFECTS OF LIGHT

Jesus said there are two things that will take place when you let your light shine. The first one is that "men will see your good deeds." In the original Greek, the word translated as *good* carries the idea of "beautiful, excellent, or handsome." In this case it implies an act that is pleasing or attractive to those who see it. Jesus says that our good works should make us attractive to those in need. When you encourage a person who is down, you are performing a good deed. When you stop and help a person who has a flat tire, you are performing a good deed. When you visit a friend in the hospital or apologize to a neighbor or stop to feed a homeless man, all of these are good deeds, and they help make Jesus attractive to people who are hurting. Others will look at your life and see the light of Jesus shining in your life, and some will desire what you have. I know for certain that it was the quality of the life that my wife, Sonia, was living that first attracted me to Christ. She didn't have to say anything. I saw the changes that took place in the way she treated people who were in need. I also saw the joy and peace she experienced while serving others. I desperately wanted what she had. That is what Jesus is getting at in this text.

There's a great poem called "The Living Sermon," by Edgar Guest, that drives this point home beautifully. Here are some excerpts:

> I'd rather see a sermon
> Than hear one any day
> I'd rather one would walk with me
> Than merely tell the way . . .
>
> The lectures you deliver
> May be very wise and true
> But I'd rather get my lessons
> By observing what you do.[42]

Secondly, Jesus said that as a result of our good works, God would receive the praise. Verse 16 says, "They praise your Father who is in heaven." Think about the ramifications of what He is saying. When you or I shine the light of Jesus through our good deeds here on earth, our Father in Heaven gets the glory. We have the ability to shift the focus of other people's eyes from earth toward heaven. That's a lot of power and influence that God has entrusted us with. By our actions we can literally point men to God, leading them out of the darkness and into His light. This is how light always works. It never shines on itself, but instead serves to illuminate

---

42   *Collected Verse of Edgar Guest* (New York: Buccaneer Books, 1976), 599.

other things. One of my favorite illustrations of this point comes from the description of the tabernacle in the Old Testament. The lamp stand was placed on a table so that its light would shine on the showbread. The showbread is a type or picture of Jesus Christ, our daily bread. When the lamp stand illuminated the showbread, the priest was reminded of God's goodness through His daily provision for our physical needs, but more importantly, through His eternal provision for our spiritual needs.

God has given us the highest calling possible. As Jesus' disciples, we are given the task of illuminating God's character and nature to a world that is desperately looking for answers. Listen to Ray Pritchard's summary, "I cannot imagine anything higher or greater. We have in our hands enormous influence for good. We are 'the light of the world.' We can make an eternal difference to the people around us. We can, quite literally, change the world. As they see the beauty of our lives, they will be attracted to the Jesus we preach. As they see the light in us, they will see the One who gives us the light. They will be attracted to our Savior, and God will get the credit."[43]

---

43   Pritchard, "Salt and Light", (online sermon).

GOING DEEPER

1) Reread Matthew 5:1–16 in its entirety. Which Beatitude stands out the most to you? Why?

2) Which Beatitude do you think you will find the most difficult to embrace in your life?

3) How important is it for you to experience the transformation that Jesus is describing in this text?

4) How has reading this chapter changed your opinion of the value and importance of salt? How about light?

5) Are you ready to begin living a life that reflects the characteristics of salt and light?

EPILOGUE

WE'VE COVERED A LOT OF ground in this book. We started with the recognition that something has gone terribly wrong in the sinful human heart. We all have a spiritual disease that is terminal. Left to our own devices, we have no hope of finding a cure. But thankfully, God in His great mercy, and through His amazing grace, has made a way for us to receive the cure. Through the life, death, and burial of Jesus Christ, God has provided us with a second chance. No longer do we have to be slaves to sin and physical death, but now we can experience the power of being raised into new life with Christ.

With this new life comes a new occupation. Our job as disciples of Jesus is to be salt and light, to influence our culture by illuminating the goodness of God through the work of His Son. And when we **don't** do our job, corruption and darkness run rampant. Here's the bottom line. The world can do nothing but get worse on its own; because it has no inherent goodness to build on, year after year, the system of evil accumulates a deeper darkness. After the Fall in the Garden of Eden and up until Genesis 6, God looked at mankind and gave His assessment: "The Lord saw how great

man's wickedness on the earth had become, and that every inclina-
tion of the thoughts of his heart was only evil all the time" (v. 5).
Everything restarted after the flood and continued until the time of
Sodom and Gomorrah. What was God's next judgment? He said
their sin was so horrendous that He must destroy them. Even after
God's first intervention with the flood, mankind did not learn its
lesson. There was a continued evil and a turning away from God.

What about after God's covenant with Abraham, and all that
has taken place through today? Certainly things are getting better.
After all, we are so much more enlightened than our ancestors. But
as we mentioned in our introduction, at the start of the twentieth
century, educators and philosophers predicted a man-made utopia,
with no war or sickness: humankind would save itself. But instead,
the twentieth century was the bloodiest century in recorded human
history. We have new diseases that are immune to our best efforts at
treatment. Mankind's increased knowledge has led to new threats
that weren't even imaginable one hundred years ago. And what is
God's assessment? We find a clue in 2 Peter 3:

> By the same word the present heavens and earth are re-
> served for fire, being kept for the day of judgment and
> destruction of the ungodly. But do not forget this one
> thing, dear friends: With the Lord a day is like a thou-
> sand years, and a thousand years are like a day. The Lord
> is not slow in keeping his promise, as some understand
> slowness. Instead he is patient with you, not wanting
> anyone to perish, but everyone to come to repentance.
> But the day of the Lord will come like a thief. The
> heavens will disappear with a roar; the elements will be

destroyed by fire, and the earth and everything done in
it will be laid bare. – 2 Pet. 3:7–10

Regardless of what educators, philosophers, scientists, and world
leaders tell us, increased knowledge does not stop the corruption.
We go from war to greater war, from crime to greater crime, from
immorality to greater immorality, from perversion to greater perversion. I saw a Facebook quote recently that openly mocked God's
word. It was posted after the state of Colorado passed two pieces of
legislation: one that legalized marijuana, and the other that changed
the definition of marriage. The post said that maybe the verse in the
Old Testament that talks about stoning a person for having sexual
relations with a person of the same sex was actually talking about
allowing them to get "stoned" on marijuana. In Romans chapter
1, Paul describes the consequences of this kind of foolish mockery:

> The wrath of God is being revealed from heaven against
> all the godlessness and wickedness of people, who suppress
> the truth by their wickedness, since what may be known
> about God is plain to them, because God has made it plain
> to them. For since the creation of the world God's invis-
> ible qualities—his eternal power and divine nature—have
> been clearly seen, being understood from what has been
> made, so that people are without excuse. For although they
> knew God, they neither glorified him as God nor gave
> thanks to him, but their thinking became futile and their
> foolish hearts were darkened. [22] Although they claimed to
> be wise, they became fools. – Rom. 1:18–22

And this leads us to a truth that is essential for us to understand: nothing good can come out of the world apart from Christ! The Church must not accept the world's self-centeredness, easy solutions, immorality, and materialism as our own standard. Not if we have any hope of becoming the salt and light that Jesus calls His followers to be! We are called to minister to the world, while being separated from its standards and ways.

In Matthew 9:12–13 Jesus says, "It is not the healthy who need a doctor, but the sick. But go and learn what this means: 'I desire mercy, not sacrifice.' For I have not come to call the righteous, but sinners." Jesus didn't come to pat self-righteous people on the back and tell them how good they are. He came to save sinners who recognize their need for God's help. That is your greatest need! That is my greatest need! And certainly, that is the world's greatest need!

The cure that Jesus offers is not a one-time pardon, but a complete life change. It is a radical transformation that takes us from brokenness to wholeness, from despair to hope, and most importantly, from death to life! Every one of us reading this book has someone we know—a family member, a friend, a neighbor, a co-worker—who is spiritually sick. Through our relationship to Jesus Christ, not only do we have access to the cure that they need, but according to Jesus, as we live for Him, as we let our light shine in the dark, we are part of how He brings the cure to bear on this lost world in which live.

For more information about
Steve Byrens
&
The Cure
please visit:

Website: www.stevebyrens.com
E-mail: sbyrens@cablespeed.com
Facebook: www.facebook.com/thecurepfl

. . . .

For more information about
AMBASSADOR INTERNATIONAL
please visit:

www.ambassador-international.com
@AmbassadorIntl
www.facebook.com/AmbassadorIntl

www.ingramcontent.com/pod-product-compliance
Lightning Source LLC
LaVergne TN
LVHW051411080426
835508LV00022B/3037